HOW TO UNDERSTAND AND USE COMPANY ACCOUNTS

Roy Warren

Partner, Sharp Parsons Tallon, Chartered Accountants

C

CENTURY
BUSINESS

Roy Warren was for many years a partner in a national firm of Chartered Accountants. He is now a partner in Sharp Parsons Tallon, a five-partner City firm which specializes in the needs of owner-managed businesses.

Published by Century Ltd
Random House, 20 Vauxhall Bridge Road, London SW1V 2SA

Random House Australia (Pty) Limited
16 Dalmore Drive, Scoresby,
Victoria 3179, Australia

Random House New Zealand Limited
18 Poland Road, Glenfield
Auckland 10, New Zealand

Random House South Africa (Pty) Limited
Endulini, 5a Jubilee Road,
Parktown, 2193, South Africa

Random House UK Limited Reg. No. 954009

Papers used by Random House UK Limited are natural, recyclable products made from wood grown in sustainable forests. The manufacturing processes conform to the environmental regulations of the country of origin.

ISBN 0 7126 7764 X   *19445679*

Typeset by Book Ens, Saffron Walden, Essex

Printed and bound in Great Britain by Butler & Tanner, Frome, Somerset

Companies, institutions and other organizations wishing to make bulk purchases of any business books published by Random House should contact their local bookseller or Random House direct:

Special Sales Director
Random House, 20 Vauxhall Bridge Road, London SW1V 2SA
tel 0171 973 9000 Fax 0171 828 6681
www.randomhouse.co.uk
businessbooks@randomhouse.co.uk

Contents

Introduction: purpose of the book

This book is written for businessmen, particularly non-accountant businessmen and those who do not have their own in-house accounting expertise. Its purpose is to provide the businessman with an understanding of his accounts, an insight into what they can tell him and how they can help him to plan for a more profitable business.

To do this we shall be looking at Dovetails Limited, a well established, medium-sized company which is in the business of making furniture.

Although a manufacturer and although medium sized, Dovetails is used as no more than a convenient vehicle for illustrating the themes of the book. The objective is to provide an explanation of accounts and the uses to which they can be put: the description in these pages applies equally to the largest of companies and the smallest of traders, and it will be as relevant to service companies as it is to those engaged in the manufacture of a tangible product.

Dovetails' accounts for 19X1 are set on the pages that immediately follow. At first sight they may make daunting reading; many businessmen may well have experienced the same sense of bewilderment – and possibly frustration – when presented with their own accounts. Before we go any further, therefore, we would do well to answer the charge 'Why bother?'. Books are rarely seen on subjects such as bridge building for the non-engineer, or pension valuations for the non-actuary – so why accounts for the non-accountant businessman? Why does a businessman *need* to understand his accounts? There are at least three compelling reasons.

- The first is that he simply cannot do without them. More than anything else, of course, a successful business depends on the flair of the businessman – and that flair in turn requires a knowledge of the product, an eye for a market, and a range of managerial skills. But no matter how good the product, or how well it is packaged, or how committed the workforce, or caring the management, a businessman only *stays* in business if he makes a profit – and the only way he knows whether he is making a profit is by drawing up a set of accounts.

- Second, accounts can do much more than that. With careful examination, they are potentially very informative documents; and by careful analysis, they can show a businessman not only whether he has made a profit but why that profit was not as good as it might have been, and how he might make it better in the future. A good businessman will not only want to make a profit, he will want to control his business, monitor its performance, and lead it to greater profitability. The surest way in which a businessman can control the performance of his business is by watching his accounts, and by listening to what they are telling him.

● Third, an understanding of accounts will lead to better business decisions. If he wants to decide whether to borrow more money from the bank, or whether to invest in new machinery, or whether to tender for a new contract, the first thing a businessman needs is a full appreciation of the business's current financial state of affairs – what its present resources are and how its existing funds are presently deployed. That can only come from an assessment of his accounts. He can be sure that his bank, or suppliers, or competitors, will themselves be looking at his accounts and making their own assessment, and the businessman is at a clear disadvantage if they understand more about the present state of his business than he does himself.

Of course, by being able to understand his own accounts the businessman will also be able to understand the accounts of other people: he can make his own assessment of whether his competitors are really as strong as they make out to be, or whether a new customer is as creditworthy as he claims, or whether a potential supplier is likely to be in business long enough to ensure a continuous source of essential materials. A proper understanding of accounts will therefore not only help a businessman to plan and control his own business but will also give him an insight into the operations of other businesses.

A final reason – and perhaps the most compelling of all – is that the understanding he needs is really not that difficult to acquire – as the following pages will hopefully show.

Outline: how to use the book

The book assumes no accounting knowledge but the layout, in three separate parts, is constructed in a way which will hopefully take those who wish to read the whole of it to a well advanced level of understanding.

As far as possible, the intention has been to avoid technical jargon and to explain the meaning and interpretation of accounts in straightforward language. That is not to say that matters of accounting concept or principle have been totally avoided: coverage is given to them in so far as they are necessary for a full understanding of the sort of information that accounts are intended to convey. Indeed, in this respect an awareness of certain of the fundamental principles on which accounts are drawn up is essential, for in many respects they act as limiting factors on the alternative uses to which accounts can be put.

This should not, therefore, be taken as a technical textbook on accounting theory, but it may nevertheless serve as a guide to a practical understanding of what accounts are all about.

Part One prepares the ground. Accounts such as Dovetails' are prepared in the first instance from underlying accounting records. In order to understand accounts we need first to understand the procedures by which business transactions are recorded. Of the two chapters in Part One, the first provides an introduction to the accounting process and explains how, for example, the technique of double entry produces a 'balance' sheet that has two equal sides.

The second chapter in Part One describes the transition from accounting records to the preparation of a set of accounts. Accounts tell a story about a business and, if the story is to be as fair and complete as possible, the raw data provided by the accounting records may need to be amended and adjusted. The way in which these amendments and adjustments are made is governed by a small number of fundamental accounting concepts. Chapter 2 describes them and underlines the degree of judgement and estimation involved in applying them. These concepts set the parameters for the story accounts are designed to tell. Anyone who really wants to understand accounts needs to understand where these parameters are drawn.

With this background, Part Two takes the reader *line by line* through Dovetails' accounts. The general purpose is to explain what the words mean and how each of the figures is arrived at. For ease of reference, the relevant extracts from the body of Dovetails' accounts are reproduced beside the paragraphs that describe and explain them. Separate chapters are devoted to the contents of the balance sheet, the profit and loss account and the cash flow statement.

By the end of Part Two the reader should have an appreciation of how accounts are made, what they mean, and the manner in which they describe the financial position and performance of a business. All of that is offered as the necessary precursor to the practical core of the book contained in Part Three, which explains how the businessman can use his accounts – and his understanding of them – to the practical benefit of his business.

Part Three explains the techniques of ratio analysis and the calculation and interpretation of key ratios are illustrated by applying them to a full analysis of Dovetails' accounts. Considerable emphasis is placed on the assessment of trends as well as the sources of comparison by which the businessman might evaluate his own performance. By this means Part Three explains how the intelligent and informed use of accounting information can help business managers chart the route to greater profitability. A separate chapter is devoted to the equally important question of business liquidity, and on the means of avoiding cash crisis. A further chapter deals with the needs of proprietory and other shareholders and describes how they can use the information provided in the accounts to assess the value of their investment, its growth, and the level of risk attaching to it.

Part Four reverts to the question of accounting principles. Its particular relevance will be to businessmen and others who are concerned to read the accounts and assess the performance of other companies. It picks up some of the accounting themes developed in earlier sections and underlines the importance of the reader being aware, when assessing a set of accounts, of how alternative accounting treatments can lead to alternative measures of profit.

DOVETAILS LIMITED

Profit and Loss Account
for the year ended 31 December 19X1

	Note	19X1 £	19X0 £
TURNOVER	2	2,424,900	1,993,400
Cost of Sales		1,786,474	1,435,856
GROSS PROFIT		638,426	557,544
Distribution Costs		98,637	72,005
Administration Costs		119,137	118,678
Other Operating Costs		264,533	209,035
OPERATING PROFIT	3	156,119	157,826
Costs incurred in closure of a factory	7	18,342	0
PROFIT ON ORDINARY ACTIVITIES BEFORE INTEREST		137,777	157,826
Interest payable	4	26,286	23,608
PROFIT ON ORDINARY ACTIVITIES BEFORE TAXATION		111,491	134,218
Tax on profit on ordinary activities	8	49,736	71,408
PROFIT FOR THE FINANCIAL YEAR		61,755	62,810
Dividends	9	21,600	20,400
RETAINED PROFIT TRANSFERRED TO RESERVES		40,155	42,410

DOVETAILS LIMITED

Balance Sheet
31 December 19X1

	Note	19X1 £	19X0 £
FIXED ASSETS			
Tangible assets	10	488,061	454,384
Investments	11	26,000	22,000
		514,061	476,384
CURRENT ASSETS			
Stock	12	435,289	404,095
Debtors		584,537	416,756
Cash		26,333	29,745
		1,046,159	850,596
CREDITORS: AMOUNTS FALLING DUE WITHIN ONE YEAR	13	641,585	452,707
NET CURRENT ASSETS		404,574	397,889
TOTAL ASSETS LESS CURRENT LIABILITIES		918,635	874,273
CREDITORS: AMOUNTS FALLING DUE AFTER MORE THAN ONE YEAR			
Long term loan	14	(140,000)	(140,000)
PROVISIONS FOR LIABILITIES AND CHARGES			
Deferred taxation	15	(99,107)	(94,900)
		679,528	639,373
CAPITAL AND RESERVES			
Called-up share capital	16	120,000	120,000
Share premium account	17	243,336	243,336
Profit and loss account	17	316,192	276,037
Revaluation reserve		–	–
		679,528	639,373

DOVETAILS LIMITED

Cash Flow Statement
for the year ended 31 December 19X1

	Note	19X1 £	19X0 £
NET CASH INFLOW FROM OPERATING ACTIVITIES	18	132,380	168,598
RETURNS ON INVESTMENTS AND SERVICING OF FINANCE	19	(26,286)	(23,608)
TAXATION		(16,299)	(12,101)
CAPITAL EXPENDITURE		(99,174)	(80,249)
EQUITY DIVIDENDS PAID		(20,400)	(18,000)
FINANCING		–	–
INCREASE IN CASH	20	(29,779)	34,640

DOVETAILS LIMITED

Notes to the accounts
year ended 31 December 19X1

1 Accounting Policies

The principal accounting policies adopted by the company in the preparation of its accounts are as follows:

(a) Depreciation

Depreciation is not charged in respect of freehold land. On other assets it is charged in equal instalments over their anticipated useful lives. The rates of depreciation used are as follows:

Freehold buildings   –   2 per cent per annum
Tools and equipment   –   15 per cent per annum
Motor vehicles   –   25 per cent per annum

(b) Stocks

Stocks and work in progress are stated at the lower of cost and net realisable value. Cost of materials is determined on a first on first out basis. For work in progress and finished goods, cost includes materials, direct labour and attributable production overhead. Net realisable value is based on estimated sales proceeds after allowing for all further costs of disposal and conversion of goods to their finished condition.

(c) Taxation

The charge for taxation is based on the profit for the year, and takes into account taxation deferred because of timing differences in the treatment of certain items for accounting and taxation purposes, but only where there is reasonably probability of payment.

2 Turnover

Turnover represents the invoiced value of goods supplied during the year, excluding value added tax. The analysis of turnover by class of business and by geographical market is as follows:

	19X1	19X0
	£	£
United Kingdom	2,308,567	1,872,867
European Community	116,333	120,533
	2,424,900	1,993,400
Domestic furniture	1,672,281	1,508,077
Office furniture	752,619	485,323
	2,424,900	1,993,400

3 Profit on ordinary activities	19X1	19X0
Profit on ordinary activities is arrived at after charging:	£	£
Directors' emoluments	43,500	42,000
Depreciation	65,404	59,926
Hire of plant and machinery	16,476	12,210
Auditors' remuneration	5,000	4,500
Staff costs (Note 6)	646,863	575,817
and after crediting:		
Income from investments		
Listed	1,078	741
Unlisted	1,200	1,000
	2,278	1,741
4 Interest payable		
Bank interest	13,686	11,008
Interest on long-term loan	12,600	12,600
	26,286	23,608
5 Analysis of profit		
The analysis of profit before tax by class of business is as follows:		
Domestic furniture	88,426	103,396
Office furniture	41,407	30,822
	129,833	134,218

	19X1 £	19X0 £
6 Staff costs		
Wages and salaries	596,062	531,952
Social security costs	50,801	43,865
	646,863	575,817

	Number of employees	
The average weekly number of employees during the year, analysed by function, was as follows:		
Works	186	202
Sales and administration	20	21
	206	223

	19X1 £	19X0 £
7 Exceptional charge		
Redundancy and other costs relating to the closure of Scunthorpe factory	37,354	–
Corporation tax relief thereon	19,012	–
	18,342	–
8 Tax on profit on ordinary activities		
Based on the profit for the year		
Corporation tax at XX%	45,015	15,538
Transfer to deferred tax	4,721	55,870
	49,736	71,408
9 Dividend		
Proposed Ordinary dividend of 18p (19X0 – 17p) per share	21,600	20,400

	Freehold Property	Tools & Equipment	Motor Vehicles	Total
	£	£	£	£
10 Tangible fixed assets				
Cost:				
At 1 Jan 19X0	227,575	391,789	35,557	654,921
Additions	50,715	43,913	6,046	100,674
Disposals	–	(18,866)	–	(18,866)
At 31 Dec 19X1	278,290	416,836	41,603	736,729
Depreciation:				
At 1 Jan 19X0	27,309	159,161	14,067	200,537
Charge for the year	5,058	50,483	9,863	65,404
Disposals	–	17,273	–	17,273
At 31 Dec 19X1	32,367	192,371	23,930	248,668
Net book values				
At 31 Dec 19X1	318,348	224,465	17,673	488,061
At 31 Dec 19X0	200,266	232,628	21,490	454,384

	19X1 £	19X0 £
Capital commitments		
Contracted for but not provided in the accounts	4,600	28,100
Authorised but not yet contracted for	8,900	1,900

11 Investments

	£
Cost:	
At 1 Jan 19X0	22,000
Additions	4,000
Disposals	–
At 31 Dec 19X1	26,000

	19X1 £	19X0 £
Listed Investments	14,000	14,000
Unlisted Investments	12,000	8,000
	26,000	22,000

Valuation:

Listed investments at market value	17,963	15,236

The Unlisted investment comprises 12,000 Ordinary shares in Legato Limited, representing 15% of the issued share capital of that company.

	19X1	19X0
	£	£
12 Stocks		
Raw materials	211,579	195,026
Work-in-progress	202,993	187,792
Finished goods	20,717	21,277
	435,289	404,095
13 Creditors		
Bank overdraft	111,966	85,599
Trade creditors	461,958	329,877
Taxation	46,061	16,831
Dividend	21,600	20,400
	641,585	452,707

The bank overdraft is secured by a fixed charge on the freehold property of the company

14 Long term loan	140,000	140,000

The unsecured loan carries interest at 9% and is repayable at the company's option between 2001 and 2005 with a final redemption date of 31 December 2005.

	£
15 Deferred taxation	
At 1 January 19X1	94,900
Transfer from profit and loss account	4,721
Adjustment to advance corporation tax	514
At 31 December 19X1	99,107

	Amounts provided	
	19X1	19X0
	£	£
Accelerated capital allowances	108,364	103,643
Advance corporation tax	9,257	8,743
	99,107	94,900

If full provision were made the potential liability would be as follows:

Accelerated capital allowances	147,500	138,000

	19X1 £	19X0 £
16 Share Capital		
Authorised		
150,000 Ordinary shares of £1 each	150,000	150,000
Allotted and fully paid:		
120,000 Ordinary shares of £1 each	120,000	120,000

	Share premium	Profit and loss account
17 Reserves		
At 1 January 19X1	243,336	276,037
Retained profit	–	40,155
At 31 December 19X1	243,336	316,192

18 Reconciliation of operating profit
to net cash inflow from operating activities

	£
Operating profit	156,119
Depreciation	65,404
Profit on sale of tangible fixed assets	3,907
Exceptional items	18,342
Increase in stocks	31,194
Increase in debtors	167,781
Increase in creditors	132,081
Net cash inflow from operating activities	132,380

19 Gross Cashflows

Returns on investments and servicing of finance:	
Interest Received	–
Interest Paid	26,286
	26,286
Capital Expenditure	
Payments to acquire tangible fixed assets	100,674
Payments to acquire trade investments	4,000
Receipts from sales of tangible fixed assets	(5,500)
	99,174

20 Analysis of changes in net debt

	1 Jan. X1 £	Cashflows £	31 Dec. X1 £
Cash in hand, at bank	29,745	(3,412)	26,333
Bank overdrafts	(85,599)	(26,367)	(111,966)
	(55,854)	(29,779)	(85,633)

Part One

CONSTRUCTION OF ACCOUNTS: HOW ARE THEY MADE?

1 The accounting process: recording business transactions

Dovetails is an ordinary, medium-sized business. Nevertheless their accounts stretch out over eight pages. They are a formidable and rather uninviting set of documents, and the businessman may well be forgiven if he dismisses them as no more than a riddle, wrapped in a mystery of technical jargon.

In Chapter 2 we shall examine the figures, and begin to unravel some of the jargon. Before we can examine the accounts in detail, however, we need to understand where they come from, and why they take the shape that they do. In particular, we need to understand the difference between the accounts as they are set out and the accounting records from which they are derived and prepared. We also need to understand the small number of fundamental principles that are applied in preparing them, for these set the parameters to the quantity and quality of information that accounts can provide. This chapter provides the necessary background. It explains how accounts are made.

THE ACCOUNTING RECORDS

Dovetails provides the vehicle for this book, so for the background we might go back ten years to the week when John Dovetail first set up in business. What happened in that first week?

JOHN DOVETAIL – BUSINESS DIARY
Jan 1 Paid in £5,000 savings
Jan 2 Bought workshop £4,000
Jan 2 Bought tools £300
Jan 3 Borrowed £1,000 from FD
Jan 3 Bought timber £100
Jan 5 Sold table £130

An examination of John Dovetail's business diary shows that on the first day he opened a business bank account and paid in his savings of £5,000. Then he bought a small workshop for £4,000, spent £300 on the tools of his trade, and borrowed £1,000 from his father (FD). Next, because he was a carpenter, he bought £100 worth of timber and set to work to make it into a table. By the end of the week the table was finished and he sold it for £130.

How did John Dovetail's business stand at the end of its first week? Although he hadn't done very much, Dovetail may have found that question difficult to answer. He could probably confirm how much he had in the bank, or what he had spent his money on day by day, but he may have found it difficult to put the whole story together. He would have found it easier if he had kept proper accounting records, but he hadn't yet discovered the accounting process of double entry.

DOUBLE ENTRY

The technique of double entry is not as mysterious as it may sound. It can be observed in everyday transactions. If a man owns a car, for example, he knows – unless he was very lucky – that he had to pay cash for it. He acquired one thing – a car – in exchange for another – cash. Alternatively, he may have borrowed the money from the bank. In that case he acquired the car in exchange for a commitment to repay the bank. There are two aspects to be observed in any transaction; double entry merely records both of them.

By keeping financial records on this basis, e.g. by recording both the acquisition of a car and the payment of cash or the acquisition of the car and the amount borrowed from the bank, the accounting process enables us to record, for each transaction, the two equal and opposite effects that it has on the financial standing of the business. And it is because the accounting process is based on double entry that a 'balance' sheet can be prepared which has two equal sides.

ASSETS, LIABILITIES AND CAPITAL: THE BALANCE SHEET

When Dovetail first set up in business, there were only two places he could have obtained the money: used his own or borrowed someone else's. He did both, and then he used the money to buy the things he needed to run the business. These simple events describe the three main components of any balance sheet:

ASSETS = what the business owns
LIABILITIES = what the business owes
CAPITAL = the owner's interest in the business

The two sides of a balance sheet arrange these components in a way which shows 'where the money came from' (on the one hand) and 'where it is now' (on the other) – see Frame 1.

Frame 1

The balance sheet equation

(Where the money came from)				(Where it is now)
CAPITAL	+	LIABILITIES	=	ASSETS

The balancing of the balance sheet results from the process of double entry. More particularly, it results from the fact that the two sides of any transaction can be recorded in terms of their effect on any one or more of these three main elements: assets, liabilities and capital.

Consider John Dovetail's first week of business. The payment of his savings into a bank account would have been recorded (from the point of view of the business) in terms of both John Dovetail's capital interest in it (£5,000) *and* the acquisition of an asset (cash £5,000). When he bought the workshop, the double entry would have been to record the acquisition of one asset (workshop £4,000) *and* the reduction in another asset (cash £4,000). Similarly when he bought tools for £300: the accounting process would have recorded both the acquisition of those tools *and* the reduction in cash he had to pay for them. The same when he borrowed money, increasing the business' cash holding by £1,000 *and* recording the liability to his father for the same amount. And again when he bought the timber: increase in one asset (timber); decrease in another (cash).

And then he worked on the timber, made it into a table and sold it for £130. The business received £130 cash, but the asset given in exchange was only in the records at £100. What has happened of course is that Dovetail has made a profit, and that is what he is in business for – to see his capital grow. Everytime he exchanges one asset for a bigger asset he makes a profit, and everytime he makes a profit his capital grows. Profits are increases in the owner's capital interest, and that is how the accounting entry for this transaction would be completed: an increase in one asset (cash £130), a decrease in another asset (timber £100), and the difference representing an increase in capital (£30).

With his records on a proper accounting basis, Dovetail can readily draw up a balance sheet to show where his business stands at the end of the first week (see Frame 2). Note that the balance sheet shows where Dovetail had

Frame 2

Dovetail's balance sheet end of first week			
Where the money came from		*Where it is now*	
	£		£
CAPITAL	5,000	ASSETS	
Profit	30	Workshop	4,000
LIABILITY	1,000	Tools	300
		Cash	1,730
	6,030		6,030

got to at the end of his first week, but not how he had got there. It shows that he had made a profit, but not how that profit was made. It says nothing about buying timber and selling furniture, but that's what his business is all about – he hopes to buy a great deal of timber and sell a great deal of furniture.

That is exactly what happened. The business flourished, and very quickly Dovetail found that he couldn't manage on his own. He employed another carpenter and as well as the wages he had to pay he was of course soon paying as well for power and light and rates for his workshop. Profit was no longer a simple comparison between the cost of timber and the price he obtained for a piece of furniture. Indeed he started buying timber in larger quantities, enough for several tables and of different qualities and length, and it became even more difficult to assess the cost of the timber that went into each piece of furniture that he sold. With all these costs to be accounted for, the calculation of profit on any one sale would be an extremely complicated exercise, and the accounting records would quickly be reduced to a state of almost indecipherable complexity.

REVENUE AND EXPENSES: THE PROFIT AND LOSS ACCOUNT

To avoid that, two further sections are introduced into the accounting records. Every time Dovetail sold a piece of furniture he recorded the increase in asset (cash) and maintained the double entry by noting that the cash came from 'sales'. And every time he incurred a cost connected with those sales, he recorded the reduction in asset (cash) and maintained the double entry by noting that the cash went on 'cost of sales'. These two further elements in the accounting process are usually described as:

REVENUE = Money received from selling the product of the business

EXPENSES = Costs incurred in making and selling that product

If from time to time total revenues are compared with total expenses, the difference will be the profit or loss which has been made not on any one

Frame 3

	£
Dovetail's profit and loss account · for first week	
REVENUE	
Sale of furniture	130
Less: EXPENSES	
Cost of timber	100
PROFIT	30

Frame 4

individual sale but on all the sales that have taken place since they were last summarised.

Extending the accounting records in this way provides the basis for preparing a profit and loss account. That for Dovetail's first week would look as in Frame 3. It summarises the results of trading during the week, and shows how the profit disclosed in the balance sheet arose.

There are now five main elements to the accounting records: assets, liabilities, capital, revenue and expense. It is important to remember, however, that profits accrue to capital; that revenue and expense are no more than sub-components of capital; and therefore that the profit and loss account is no more than a sub-analysis of the capital section of the balance sheet. This can be illustrated by extending the balance sheet equation as shown in Frame 4.

Alternatively, the equation can be rearranged in simplified form as follows:

Capital = Assets – Liabilities

The right-hand side of this equation (assets – liabilities) is often described as 'net assets', and this form of expression provides the basis for the accounting description of profit (an increase in capital) as representing an increase in net assets.

These five components provide the framework for keeping full and comprehensive accounting records. Any business transaction, no matter what its apparent complexity, can be described and recorded in terms of its effect on assets, liabilities, capital, revenue or expense; and the double-entry process keeps the equation constantly in balance by recording the dual aspects to any transaction in terms of their effect in increasing or decreasing any one or more of these five main elements.

Accounting records also provide the means by which day-by-day control can be exercised over the affairs of the business, and for this purpose the businessman will want his records in as much detail as possible. Dovetail

Frame 5

ASSETS	£	LIABILITIES	£	CAPITAL	£
Workshop	4,000	Loan from FD	1,000	J. Dovetail	5,000
Tools	300				
Cash	3,985				

REVENUE	£	EXPENSES	£
Sales of furniture	5,350	Materials	1,260
		Labour	970
		Overheads	835

Frame 6

Dovetail's profit and loss account for first year

	£	£
REVENUE		
Sale of furniture		5,350
Less: EXPENSES		
Materials	1,260	
Labour	970	
Overheads	835	
		3,065
Profit		2,285

Dovetail's balance sheet at the end of the first year

CAPITAL		ASSETS	
Capital	5,000	Workshop	4,000
Profit	2,285	Tools	300
	7,285	Cash	3,985
LIABILITY			
Loan	1,000		
	8,285		8,285

would want to know not just how much his expenses were in total, but how much he was spending on timber, or electricity, or wages. So he would keep not just one cost of sales account but several expense accounts – according to the nature of the expenses he incurred. Similarly, he will want separate records for each of the business' assets, and separate details, for example, of transactions with each person to whom he might owe money, or who might owe money to him. Accounting records will become detailed in their analysis, but no matter how extensive or sophisticated they might be they will always be organised under these five main categories – and it is because of this ordering of the accounting process that accounts take the shape that they do.

Frame 5 summarises Dovetail's accounting records as they stood at the end of his first year of business. Of course, these figures are not the records themselves but totals extracted from the records, representing in some cases the accumulation of several hundred entries made during the year to record the several hundred transactions that Dovetail entered into. It is these totals, however, which provide the basis from which we can prepare accounts. The profit and loss account set out in Frame 6 compares Dovetail's sales with his expenses to reveal that as a result of all of his trading activities during the year Dovetail had made a profit of £2,285; and the balance sheet which follows shows that at the end of the first year the business had assets totalling £8,285, owed liabilities totalling £1,000, and that Dovetail's capital interest had been increased from its original £5,000 by the profit of £2,285.

2 Preparing accounts: describing a business

The process of summarisation draws out the essential difference between keeping accounting records and preparing a set of accounts. The records are rather like a diary: look up any one page and you will find all the detail you need about each event and transaction that took place. But, like a diary, accounting records have the same limitations: they only provide the detail of each event; they don't draw the events together.

Accounts condense and summarise the information contained in the records into the form of a story. The story has two main chapters: the balance sheet, which assembles information in answer to the question 'Where are we?'; and the profit and loss account, which attempts to answer the question 'How did we get here?'. (Later on, we shall come to a further chapter – the cash flow statement – which explains a little about 'What happened on the way?')

Unfortunately, the process – from accounting records to accounts – is not quite that straightforward. Anyone looking inside John Dovetail's workshop on the last day of the year would find a supply of unused timber – timber which Dovetail has had to pay money for, and which is included in the cost of materials in his profit and loss account. But that timber is not an expense of this year's sales – it will go into furniture that he hopes to sell next year. Similarly with the tables which are not quite finished – are they not as much an asset of the business at the end of the year as the workshop and tools are? And the bill outstanding for the latest supply of materials, or the amount due to carpenters for the last week's wages – are they not liabilities of the business at the year end?

The answer to all these questions is, of course, yes. The point is that the accounting records do not necessarily contain all the information needed to prepare accounts. If the story told in the accounts is to be as fair and complete as possible, the raw information provided by the accounting records may need to be amended and adjusted. The need arises because, whereas the activities of the business continue from day to day, the act of preparing accounts happens only occasionally: in order to prepare them, we have to 'freeze' the flow of the business – rather like taking a still frame from a moving picture. We split the life of a business into periods, usually of one year, and in this act we move from the exact science of noting transactions in the accounting records to the rather more imprecise art of describing the financial position of a business and measuring its profit to date.

This process will often involve a considerable degree of estimation and opinion. (If Dovetail's half-finished tables, for example, are to be regarded as an asset of the business at the end of the year, what cost should be attributed to them?) In order to provide some consistency in the estimates that are made, and to provide a framework within which to exercise their judgement, accountants have adopted a number of generally accepted principles and conventions. Some of these are specific and are concerned with particular types of asset, revenue or expense. Others are more wide-ranging in their effect and it is these we shall look at in the remainder of this chapter. Their importance is that they imply certain assumptions about what accounts are and are not intended to convey. If we want to understand accounts, we need to understand these conventions. And if we want to make use of the information contained in accounts, we need to understand the degree of estimation that goes into preparing them.

'REALISATION', OR HOW TO MEASURE REVENUE

There are only a small handful of broad rules that we need to be concerned with. The first is the principle of realisation. Its effect can be observed in the results that were reported for John Dovetail's first week in business.

We said then that he had made a profit because he had *sold* a table, but Dovetail might well claim (and most economists would agree with him) that he started to earn that profit as soon as he started to *make* the table, and that the earning process continued during the making of it. In terms of economic theory that is no doubt true; for accounting purposes, however, it would be impractical to attempt to calculate how much profit was earned on each of the three days it took to make the table – even if we could reasonably assume in advance what the total amount of the eventual profit was likely to be. Such a measure would be too subjective, and open to widely differing estimates and interpretations. For accounting purposes the measure of revenue needs to be objective, and so we adopt the principle of realisation: a profit isn't recognised until it is 'realised' in the form of a sale.

There are certain extreme circumstances in which this rule has to be bent. An engineering company, for example, might take four years to build a bridge, and it would clearly be a distortion to allocate all of its profit to the fourth year and none to the first three. For this reason there are exceptional rules which apply when accounting for long-term contracts; but they are the exception. The general rule remains: profit is not recognised until the earning process has been completed and a sale has been made.

'HISTORIC COST', OR HOW TO MEASURE ASSETS: 1

The convention by which accounts are based on historic (or original) costs is the mirror image of the realisation principle. The consequence of not recognising a profit until the point of sale is that, while they are still held, assets will always be shown in accounts at a figure based on their original cost.

Thus Dovetail's half-finished tables – his work-in-progress – will be shown at cost – even though the tables are very nearly complete. The supply of timber he bought a year ago will, if unused, be shown in his balance sheet at the end of the year at its original cost – even if its price has doubled in the meantime. The saw bench he is still using will be shown in this year's accounts at a figure which is based on the amount it cost him many years ago – even though it might cost him three or four times as much if he wanted to buy it now.

It is therefore important to appreciate that the amount at which assets are shown in the balance sheet does not necessarily represent their current value, nor what it would cost to replace them, nor what they could be sold for. Under conventional accounting, assets are shown at the historic cost of acquiring or producing them.

The twin principles of historic cost and realisation have important consequences for an understanding of accounts. Consider two garage owners, Bill and Ben. Both start the week with 100 gallons of petrol in their tanks, and both have paid £1 a gallon for it. On Tuesday, the price of petrol doubles. Bill thinks it might go up further, and decides to hold on to his stock. Ben sells, and invests the whole of the proceeds in bicycles. On Wednesday the price of bicycles doubles, as does the price of petrol once again. Bill still decides to hold on. Ben sells his bicycles and invests the whole of the proceeds (£400) back into petrol – which now costs him £4 a gallon. On Friday they both draw up their accounts. Bill's show no profit, and assets of £100. Ben's reveal a profit of £300 and assets worth £400. Yet they both started and ended the week in identical positions – with 100 gallons of petrol in their tanks.

The difference is, of course, that Ben entered into two market transactions during the week: he made two sales, and he therefore realised an accounting profit. Nevertheless, his wealth in 'real' terms at the end of the week was identical to Bill's.

The example illustrates how the principles of realisation and historic cost act as limiting factors on the type of information that accounts are intended to convey. An appreciation of them will serve the businessman well when he comes to consider such questions as the value of his business and its profitability.

'MATCHING', OR HOW TO MEASURE EXPENSE

Profit is the difference between the total revenue of a business and its total expenses for a given period. The purpose of the 'matching' principle is to ensure that, in arriving at that profit, revenue is compared or matched with *all* of the costs that have been incurred in earning it.

The matching process is sometimes referred to as the 'accruals' basis of accounting. This is merely to differentiate it from a simple cash basis, and it means that expenses should be recognised in the period in which they are incurred, rather than that in which money happens to be paid for them.

It is quite clear, for example, that if it costs £1,000 a year to rent a warehouse, then there is an expense of £1,000 to be recognised each year, regardless of how and when the rent is paid. If it was paid in lump sums of three years, £2,000 should, at the end of the first year, be carried forward as an asset – ready to be matched against the revenues of Years 2 and 3. It would be quite wrong to charge the whole of that payment as an expense of Year 1. Similarly the power used in the last quarter of a year is an expense of that year's trading – even though the electricity bill might not be paid until the following year.

The matching process does not create any difficulty when the expense is identifiable with a particular period of time. But that is not always the case. A large-scale advertising campaign, paid for this year, might be expected to boost sales over the next two or three years. How much of that cost to recognise as an expense of Year 1, and how much to carry forward and match against the revenues of Years 2 and 3 is a matter of judgement, involving a good degree of estimation.

Much the same principle applies to plant and machinery. John Dovetail might hope that his saw bench will last for many years, and its use will therefore contribute to several years' revenue. But it won't last for ever, and one way or the other its cost has to be allocated against the revenues it helps to earn. He might expect it to last eight years, in which case one eighth of its cost will be charged against the revenues of each of those years. This process is what is usually referred to as depreciation, but essentially it is no more than a further element in the matching process – the attempt to compare revenues with *all* the costs incurred in earning them.

'GOING CONCERN', OR HOW TO MEASURE ASSETS: 2

The idea of 'going concern' is not so much a principle of accounting as a general assumption which supports other, more specific, accounting procedures. The assumption made is that, in the absence of any evidence to the contrary, the business will continue to operate in the future and in the same trade. This may not of itself appear particularly startling, but the assumption of the going concern lends support, for example, to the historic cost basis of valuing assets. If we can assume that the business will continue to operate in future years, it will be appropriate to carry assets forward at their full cost; and it will therefore be unnecessary – indeed inappropriate – to state these assets at what might be a much lower disposal or break-up value.

Take for example the production of this book, and assume it to be in the course of production at the publishing company's year end. It started off life as sheets of clean and rather costly paper, which were then cut up into smaller pieces for printing. At the year-end it comprised a collection of half-printed pages, worth no more than scrap value – and certainly worth far less than the original clean sheets of paper. But by assuming a going concern, we assume that the company will continue in business next year, will finish printing and binding the book, and will sell it at a price which (in normal circumstances) would recover all the costs that have gone into it. So at the year end the going-concern assumption allows the half-processed paper to be carried forward not at its scrap value but at an amount based on the full costs incurred to date, including all the material and production costs that have so far gone into it.

Alternatively, take the table which John Dovetail had only half-finished on the last day of the year. The original length of timber from which he was making it had considerable value, but now he has sawn it, drilled it and chiselled it, although it hasn't yet taken the shape of a table. It lies around his workshop as a collection of odd bits of wood – suitable for the fire but, in their present shape, not much else. But we don't value it as firewood, we value it at the full costs that have so far been put into it – because we assume that he will finish making it, and sell it, and recover all of those costs next year.

ALLOCATING COSTS TO ACCOUNTING PERIODS

In other words the unfinished table is regarded as an asset. The costs that have gone into it will not be written off as an expense of past trading but will be reflected in the balance sheet, and carried forward to be written off next year and matched against the revenue to be derived from its sale.

This illustrates a theme which is central to the preparation of accounts: whether costs – regardless of how they are described in the records – are properly regarded, for the purpose of preparing accounts, as assets to be carried forward or expenses to be written off. If we could have waited a week or so before preparing Dovetail's accounts, there would have been no problem – the revenue from the sale of the table would automatically have fallen in the same period as the costs of making it. If we could have waited eight years, all the costs of the sawbench would have been used up and automatically matched against the total revenue generated during those eight years. But accounts have to be prepared at least annually, and the allocation of costs to the appropriate accounting periods is one of the finer arts involved in their preparation – and one which will often involve a good deal of estimation.

'PRUDENCE', OR HOW TO ESTIMATE

The last of the conventions we need to consider – prudence – is more an attitude than a principle of accounting. Prudence says that whenever you have to exercise judgement, or make an estimate, or assess an uncertain outcome, take the pessimistic view.

We can see prudence in the principle of realisation: don't take a profit until it is certain, until it is realised in the form of a sale. More particularly, we can see it in the converse, in the rule which says provide for all known losses – whether they are realised or not. So Bill the garage owner was not able to show any profit because he hadn't sold any petrol, even though he knew he could sell it for £4 per gallon. But if the price of petrol had halved instead of doubled twice, prudence would have required that Bill's stock be written down to 25p per gallon. He would have shown a loss for the week, even though he hadn't sold anything.

Prudence has its roots in the purpose that accounts have traditionally served in providing financial information about a business to creditors, shareholders and other interested parties who, of necessity, do not have day-by-day control over the credit they have given or the money they have invested. For these purposes there is some virtue in adopting conventions such as prudence in order to temper the terms of uninhibited optimism in which management might otherwise be inclined to report. But prudence does imply 'at least as good' rather than 'most likely' or 'at best'. It does tend, on balance, towards a relative understatement of both profits and asset values, and it adds a further dimension to our understanding of accounts.

SUMMARY

To understand accounts we need to understand their derivation. Accounts are derived from accounting records, and accounting records – the means by which a business keeps a record of the transactions it has engaged in – are maintained on the basis of double entry.

The process of double entry results in a balance sheet that has two equal sides, which describe and compare assets (what the business owns) with liabilities (what the business owes) and capital (the owners' interest in the business). The balance sheet is a statement of financial position: it describes where the business stands at any given time.

The process of double entry also leads to the profit and loss account, which compares the revenues and expenses of a business for a given period. Profit is represented by an increase in net assets, and the making of a profit results in an increase in the owner's capital interest. The profit and loss account summarises how that increase arose; it analyses the movement in the capital part of the balance sheet equation. A balance sheet shows where a business stands; the profit and loss account shows how it came to stand there.

In order to make use of accounts we also need to understand the bases on which they are drawn up. A summary of the accounting records provides the starting point but, because the act of preparing accounts requires the flow of business transactions to be frozen, figures extracted from the records will need amendment and adjustment if the balance sheet is to provide a fair picture of the financial position of the business and if the profit and loss account is to provide a fair measure of its performance to date.

The process of transformation – from accounting records to a set of accounts – is one that involves accountants in a good deal of estimation and opinion. The rules that govern the estimates which are made are dominated by a sense of prudence: the principle of realisation gives a prudent measure of profit; the convention of historic cost normally results in a prudent measure of assets.

These rules serve their purpose in providing a framework in which accounts can be drawn up on a reasonably objective basis; but they also serve as limiting factors on the type of information that accounts are intended to convey. An appreciation of them is essential for an understanding of the uses to which accounts can be put.

Part Two

CONTENT OF ACCOUNTS: WHAT DO THEY MEAN?

3 Introduction

In Part Two the accounts of Dovetails Limited will be examined in detail. Since its modest beginnings, John Dovetail's furniture business has expanded considerably. Others have joined him in forming a company, which has been trading successfully for a number of years.

The company's accounts for 19X1 are set out on pages xi to xix. They comprise two things – words and figures. Our purpose in this chapter will be to look at what the words mean, and how the figures are arrived at.

First, however, it should be emphasised that the accounts reproduced are extracts from the company's published annual accounts. Because they are extracted from the published accounts, they are drawn up in a manner that complies both with the Companies Act and with Accounting Standards issued by the accounting profession.

Traditionally, the accounting requirements of the Companies Acts have sought to establish the minimum amount of information that should be included in accounts, and the format in which it should be presented: more recently, company law has also been concerned with how the figures are arrived at. Accounting Standards also regulate disclosure, but their main purpose is to establish the principles by which certain of the figures are calculated. Although, for the most part, there will be no need here to refer to the detailed requirements of either the Companies Act or the Standards, the reader should be aware of their governing influence on the accounts to be examined.

It should also be noted that in addition to the statements that are reproduced here, Dovetails' full set of published accounts would include two further reports: one by the directors and one by the auditors. The first provides a narrative commentary by the directors on the company's activities during the year (usually in rather cryptic form), but is otherwise concerned to disclose details to the outside world about the directors themselves and their interests in the company. The second report contains confirmation from the auditors that they have carried out an independent examination of the company's accounts, and includes their opinion as to whether the accounts provide a 'true and fair view' of both the company's financial position and its reported profit or loss for the year.

The accounts are in four parts: a balance sheet, a profit and loss account, a cash flow statement and supporting notes. Earlier sections described how the balance sheet and profit and loss account are derived from the accounting records. Later, we shall examine how the cash flow statement provides a re-analysis of this information in different terms.

The fourth part to the accounts – the notes – serves two purposes. First they are the traditional means of disclosing more detailed information than can reasonably be included on the face of the balance sheet or the profit and loss account. The notes can be very useful in the explanation and supporting information they provide; indeed they will often contain information which is critical for a full understanding of the main accounts. Secondly, the notes will disclose the accounting treatments adopted by the company in areas where alternative treatments would have a significant effect on the figures. For our purposes in 'walking through' the accounts of Dovetails Limited, we shall be looking at each item in the accounts in conjunction with any notes which support it.

4 The balance sheet

The balance sheet is a statement of position. It attempts to provide the financial answer to the question 'Where does the business stand?'. The first point to be noticed about a balance sheet, therefore, is that it is drawn up at a particular moment in time – in Dovetails' case, at the close of business on 31 December 19X1.

We have already noted that the business itself does not of course 'stop' on 31 December. Its trading activities are continuous. If the preparation of a balance sheet is to be compared to the taking of a still frame from a moving picture, we should also note that if we take the frame a moment earlier or a moment later, the picture will be different. In the case of the financial picture in a balance sheet, any difference will depend on the extent to which the business has engaged in any transactions of unusual significance during the days and weeks immediately surrounding the date of the balance sheet. In normal circumstances, assuming a steady pattern to the flow and terms of trading, the difference may only be marginal, and we can usually regard the balance sheet not only as a summary of affairs 'as at the balance sheet date', but also as a reasonable representation of the company's affairs on or around that date.

The second general point to note about Dovetails' balance sheet is that it is really two balance sheets, presented under the columns 19X1 and 19X0. The amounts appearing under the 19X0 column are referred to as 'comparative figures' or 'corresponding amounts' and they summarise the position as it stood on the same date last year. Their inclusion is a legal requirement, but they also provide a very useful basis for comparison: it is one thing to know where the business stands on 31 December 19X1, but it is much more useful to be able to assess that position in the context of where the business has come from. The comparative figures show where the business was twelve months ago.

Thirdly, it will be noted that Dovetails' balance sheet is presented in a vertical format. This presentation differs only in shape from the simple examples of horizontal balance sheets that were illustrated in Part One. The substance of the two formats is the same: the totals of Dovetails' vertical presentation (£679,528) retain the same, essential balance sheet equation.

FIXED ASSETS

Beneath the summary heading 'fixed assets', the first line of Dovetails' balance sheet shows tangible assets of £488,061 (and £454,384 for the previous year). The one characteristic that distinguishes a 'fixed' asset is that it is held because the business intends to use it rather than sell it.

Frame 7

10 Tangible fixed Assets	Freehold property	Tools & equipment	Motor vehicles	Total
	£	£	£	£
Cost:				
At 1 Jan 19X1	227,575	391,789	35,557	654,921
Additions	50,715	43,913	6,046	100,674
Disposals	–	(18,866)	–	(18,866)
At 31 Dec 19X1	278,290	416,836	41,603	736,729
Depreciation:				
At 1 Jan 19X1	27,309	159,161	14,067	200,537
Charge for the year	5,058	50,483	9,863	65,404
Disposals	–	(17,273)	–	(17,273)
At 31 Dec 19X1	32,367	192,371	23,930	248,668
Net book value:				
At 31 Dec 19X1	245,923	224,465	17,673	488,061
At 31 Dec 19X0	200,266	232,628	21,490	454,384

Tangible fixed assets are those which a business intends to retain for a number of years, and put to use repeatedly in the production and distribution of its products. They will normally comprise buildings in which to make and store the product, plant and machinery to make it with, and vehicles to deliver it in.

A breakdown of Dovetails' tangible fixed assets is given in Note 10 to the accounts and reproduced in Frame 7. It shows that Dovetails have three main categories of fixed assets and (in the penultimate line) that the balance sheet figure of £488,061 is made up of freehold property (£245,923), tools and equipment (£224,465) and motor vehicles (£17,673). These amounts are described in the note as being the 'net book value' of the respective assets, and it can be seen that net book value comes from a comparison of cost and depreciation. Depreciation has been touched on in Part One where it was described as the means by which the cost of a fixed asset is allocated over the various accounting periods that benefit from its use. In so doing the attempt is to match the revenues for a period with the proportion of the cost of fixed assets which is used up in earning them. The amount described as net book value represents the proportion of cost which has not yet been charged against the revenues of past periods, and which is therefore carried forward at the end of 19X1 to be allocated against the revenues of future periods.

A closer examination of the note shows that at the beginning of the year Dovetails has tools and equipment, for example, which had cost a total of £391,789. During the year the company bought further tools and equipment at a cost of £43,913, and it disposed of items which had originally cost £18,866. That left £416,836 as the total, accumulated, historic cost of the tools and equipment that Dovetails owned at the end of the year.

The next line reveals that, of the total cost of £391,789 at 1 January 19X1, £159,161 (approximately 40 per cent) had already been allocated to previous accounting periods. Of that amount, £17,273 was in respect of assets which had been disposed of during the year, and this amount is eliminated from the depreciation column in the same way as the cost of £18,866 was eliminated from the cost column. (The difference of £1,593 represents the net book value of the tools and equipment disposed of, and would be compared with the proceeds to establish whether a profit or loss was made on disposal.)

The amount of depreciation charged for 19X1 is £50,483. This represents Dovetails' estimate of the proportion of the cost of these assets which has been used up in the course of 19X1's production. As a result, the total accumulated depreciation at 31 December 19X1 amounts to £192,371. In summary, the tools and equipment that Dovetails owned at the end of 19X1 originally cost them £416,836, of which £192,371 has been written off and charged as expenses in the years up to and including 19X1, leaving unexpired costs, or net book value, to be carried forward at 31 December 19X1 of £224,465.

Note 10 provides similar information in respect of Dovetails' two other categories of fixed asset – property and vehicles – and each of these columns can be read in the same way. The relationship between cost and accumulated depreciation can give an indication as to the relative age of the assets in question: the greater the proportion that accumulated depreciation bears to original cost, the older the assets are likely to be (and the sooner they might need replacing). That assessment, however, will also require a reading of the company's depreciation policy.

DEPRECIATION

There are a number of alternative methods by which annual depreciation can be estimated, and a company can choose whichever method it believes most appropriate for allocating the cost of a fixed asset against the revenues derived from using it.

Ideally, depreciation would be charged on a usage basis. The cost of a lorry which had an expected life of 100,000 miles would be allocated to accounting periods proportionately to the number of miles travelled each year. Similarly, the cost of a machine which is expected to produce 40,000 units would be charged according to the number of units produced each year. More usually, the assumption is made that from year to year the level of business activity will be reasonably consistent, and depreciation is therefore more often charged on a straightforward time basis.

The simplest and most widely adopted method is to spread the cost of an asset in equal instalments over its expected useful life (the 'straight-line' method of depreciation). Dovetails might expect a wood-turning machine to last 8 years. If it cost £16,000, annual depreciation on a straight-line basis would be £2,000 (1/8th × £16,000) each year. At the end of year one, the machine would be shown in the balance sheet as follows:

Cost	£16,000
Less: Accumulated depreciation	2,000
	£14,000

At the end of five years, £2,000 having been written off each year, the machine would be shown in the balance sheet at a net book value of £6,000, as follows:

Cost	£16,000
Less: Accumulated depreciation	10,000
	£6,000

Whatever method of depreciation is adopted, it will be based on estimates and expectations, and circumstances can of course change in a way which makes previous estimates and expectations no longer appropriate. For example, heavily carved table legs can go out of fashion, and the wood-turning machine that is used to make them will fall idle. In that case the depreciation policy would have to be revised. The full costs of that machine can no longer be expected to be recovered, and prudence would require that its net book value should immediately be written down – either to its scrap value or to the small proportion of its cost which can reasonably be expected to be recovered from its limited future use.

Depreciation is an expense – often a highly significant one – and, because of the degree of estimation it involves, the method of calculation will usually be found in the notes to the accounts. In Dovetails' case this explanation is given in Note 1(a) – see Frame 8. This note explains that Dovetails do not charge depreciation on freehold land. That is quite usual: land does not depreciate however much it is used – it lasts for ever. On other fixed assets Dovetails charge depreciation on the straight-line basis, i.e. they allocate the cost in equal amounts over the number of years the respective assets are expected to last. The remainder of the note reveals that Dovetails expect their buildings to last 50 years (2 per cent per annum), that they expect their tools and equipment to last, on average, between 6 and 7 years (15 per cent per annum) and that they expect their vehicles to last four years (25 per cent per annum).

We might attempt to confirm this information by referring back to the line in the fixed asset note which shows the depreciation charge for the year.

Frame 8

1 *(a)   Depreciation*

Depreciation is not charged in respect of freehold land. On other assets it is charged in equal annual instalments over their anticipated useful lives. The rates of depreciation used are as follows:

Freehold buildings	– 2 per cent per annum
Tools and equipment	– 15 per cent per annum
Motor vehicles	– 25 per cent per annum

The charge for freehold property (£5,058) represents approximately 1.8 per cent of the total cost at 31 December 19 X1 of £278,290. The shortfall is due to the element of land included in the cost but which is not depreciated. The charge for tools and equipment (£50,483) represents approximately 12 per cent of the cost of £416,836. This is less than the quoted 15 per cent, and there could be a number of reasons. It may be that Dovetails calculate depreciation on a monthly basis, in which case the additions during the year of £43,913 would have suffered less than a full year's depreciation charge. Or it could be that included in the cost of tools and equipment are items that are more than seven years old, the cost of which would have been wholly written off in previous years and for which there will therefore be no depreciation to charge for the current year. Without knowing this detail we cannot reconcile the depreciation charge exactly, but the fixed asset note will often provide a broad indication of the age of the assets in question. If the charge for the year is considerably less than the quoted rate, the indication is that the assets are relatively old, and have lasted longer than was originally expected.

Depreciation is sometimes referred to, rather misleadingly, as a means of providing for the replacement of the assets in question. It is true that charging depreciation annually against profits will, over the years, ensure that funds are retained in the business equivalent to the original cost of the asset. But a fixed asset can be replaced only if there is sufficient cash – or borrowing power – available to meet the replacement cost. Depreciation can only be said to 'provide' for replacement if the funds that have been retained are kept in liquid form.

More importantly, depreciation only ensures the retention of funds amounting to the *original* cost of the asset and, even if the cash is available, it will often not be enough to buy a replacement. Referring to Dovetails' fixed asset note, it might reasonably – although not necessarily – be presumed that this year's additions to tools and equipment, which cost £43,913, were replacements for the items disposed of during the year which originally cost only £18,866. Even if that cost has been fully written off (which it has not) the accumulated annual depreciation would clearly have fallen very far short of the amount now needed for replacement. For these reasons, the annual depreciation charge is best regarded as no more than one aspect of the general principle of matching – the allocation of the cost of an asset over appropriate accounting periods. Planning for replacement is a matter of quite separate financial policy.

FIXED ASSET VALUATION

Dovetails have followed normal practice in showing their fixed assets at historic cost, less the proportion of that cost so far written off. However, because fixed assets will usually be several years old, the historic costs will usually be several years out of date. We have seen that this can have important consequences when Dovetails come to make internal plans for plant replacement. It could also have important consequences for any external assessment that might be made of the company's fixed asset position.

Dovetails' buildings, for example, will probably be worth far more – in terms of what they would fetch on the property market – than their book value of £245,923. Buildings usually last a long time; they will often have been acquired many years ago; and their book value, based on original cost, will usually be a considerable understatement of their current worth. Although it is an established principle that accounts do not purport to show disposal values, the inclusion of buildings at original cost can cause a particularly acute distortion in the balance sheet's attempt to describe the current financial position of the business. For this reason it has become a common practice for companies to include property at its current market value.

Although this represents an exception to the general principle of historic cost, it should be noted that there is no corresponding exception to the principle of realisation. If a property is revalued, the surplus that arises is unrealised, and cannot therefore be regarded as a profit. It only becomes realised – and therefore recognisable in the profit and loss account – when it is sold. The surplus does nevertheless represent an increase in asset value and, as such, is properly regarded as an increase – albeit an unrealised increase – in the proprietors' or shareholders' interest in the business. Company law requires any such unrealised uplift in value to be shown as a separate revaluation reserve on the face of the balance sheet.

INVESTMENTS

The next line in Dovetails' balance sheet shows investments of £26,000. There can be any number of reasons why a business might want to hold investments. They may represent money that has been put to one side, ready for when the time comes to replace some fixed assets. Or they may represent no more than a temporary investment of surplus cash. Their purpose will usually dictate the way in which they are disclosed in the balance sheet. In Dovetails' case, they are not shown under the general

Frame 9

11 Investments		£
Cost:		
At 1 Jan 19X1		22,000
Additions		4,000
Disposals		–
At 31 Dec 19X1		26,000

	19X1 £	19X0 £
Listed investments	14,000	14,000
Unlisted investments	12,000	8,000
	26,000	22,000
Valuation:		
Listed investments at market value	17,963	15,236

The unlisted investment comprises 12,000 ordinary shares in Legato Limited, representing 15% of the issued share capital of that company.

heading of current assets – which implies that there is no intention to sell them in the near future.

Investments can also take a variety of forms. In the examples cited, they would usually take the form of marketable securities which could be sold as soon as the funds were needed for the required purpose. Alternatively the investment might be made for purposes connected with the trade. Further details about Dovetails' investments are given in Note 11 – see Frame 9.

Dovetails have two types of investment. Listed investments are investments in companies which have a listing on the Stock Exchange. They cost Dovetails £14,000 but, because they are readily marketable, the note also shows their market value, i.e. the amount that could have been obtained for them if they had been sold on 31 December 19X1.

Dovetails also have an unlisted investment, which is shown at cost of £12,000. The note goes on to say that Dovetails have acquired a 15 per cent interest in the business of Legato Limited. There can be a variety of reasons for such trade investments. It might have been to secure benefits for Dovetails' own business operations, e.g. to secure preferential delivery from an important supplier. Or it may be simply an investment in the potential of an unrelated business. Whatever the case, trade investments should clearly be assessed quite separately from listed securities, for they usually involve a quite different degree of risk.

CURRENT ASSETS

Dovetails have three types of current asset: stock and work-in-progress; debtors; and cash. In Dovetails' case, stock will represent a supply of timber ready to be turned into furniture (raw materials), furniture which is in the course of production at the balance sheet date (work-in-progress), and furniture that is awaiting delivery to customers (finished goods). Debtors represent amounts due from customers in respect of past sales. The distinguishing feature of any asset listed as 'current' is that it is either already in the form of cash or can be expected to be turned into cash in the near future, usually one year.

The transformation into cash may take a number of months – according to the type of current asset in question. Dovetails might expect most of their debtors, for example, to pay within the next month. They might expect to deliver a good proportion of their finished goods stock, and collect payment from customers, over the next two or three months. It will take somewhat longer to process the raw materials, turn them into finished goods, sell them and collect the money. But by grouping these assets all under the heading of 'current', the implication is that, one way or the other, they can all be turned into cash within the next twelve months.

Note that the distinction between fixed and current assets depends not on the type of asset but on the type of business that is buying or selling it. Furniture is Dovetails' trading stock, but the company that buys it might expect to use it as office equipment for several years, and in its own accounts will therefore describe it as a fixed asset. Dovetails describe their delivery trucks as fixed assets, but they would have been a current asset of British Leyland (whose business it is to make and sell lorries) before they sold them to Dovetails. Similarly Dovetails' sawbench – which they hope to use for many years – would have been the trading stock of the manufacturer, Black & Decker.

Note also that the grouping of assets under the general headings of 'fixed' or 'current' is no more than a technique adopted in the preparation of a balance sheet, a technique that provides a helpful means of describing the financial position on a given date. In the days and weeks and months which follow 31 December, Dovetails will continue to make furniture, sell it, and collect money from customers. The debtors at 31 December which are turned into cash will be replaced by other debtors, and the stock which is sold will be replaced by other stock as it is produced. The business cycle continues, and phrases such as 'fixed' and 'current' only arise because of the freeze that is put on a business in order to prepare accounts.

STOCK AND WORK-IN-PROGRESS

Trading stock is the lifeblood of any business, and it is frequently one of the most significant figures in a balance sheet. It is significant in terms of its size, in the degree of estimation that is often involved in its calculation, and in the critical impact it can have on the story told by the accounts. It is also the figure which is most susceptible to error – or manipulation.

In normal circumstances, the costs of materials, wages and overheads incurred in the course of production during the year will be recorded as expenses. The calculation of stock is no more than an application of the matching principle, requiring an assessment of the proportion of those costs which should properly be regarded as an asset to be carried forward to the following year and matched against the revenues which will be generated when those goods are sold. The significance of stock in accounting terms results primarily from the estimates and assumptions that are involved in these calculations. It becomes doubly important because – as we shall see later – an increase or decrease in the value of closing stock and work-in-progress results in a corresponding increase or decrease in the profit for the year.

Because of its significance, many companies will keep subsidiary records to control the amounts and movement of stock. These records will usually be in terms of both quantities and values: entries will be made whenever raw materials are acquired, whenever they are moved to the production line, and whenever they are issued back to the shelves as finished goods. In their more sophisticated forms, such stock records will also record the labour and overhead costs that go into stock at each stage of the production process. Although they do not play a part in the double entry on which the main financial records are based, stock records do provide a good means of control and, where they exist, they will clearly provide the basis for calculating the amount of stock and work-in-progress on hand at any one time.

Where they do not exist – and Dovetails is a case in point – some other means has to be found of calculating stock and work-in-progress at the balance sheet date, and this is usually done by going into the factory or warehouse and counting what's there. That will give quantities, but the accounts, of course, are based on values, and it is the valuing of stock – the allocation of costs between items sold and items still on hand – that gives rise to the main area of estimation.

Note 12 to the accounts (see Frame 10) shows Dovetails' total stocks of £435,289 to be made up of raw materials £211,579, work-in-progress £202,993 and finished goods £20,717. Because of the principle of historic cost, the stated value of these assets will be based on the costs incurred in acquiring them or, in the case of work-in-progress and finished goods, on the costs that have been incurred into bringing them to their present state. The problem remains of establishing exactly what the 'cost' was.

Suppose that Dovetails had bought 10,000 metres of a certain type of timber evenly during the year. In the first half of the year the timber had cost 95p per metre. By the second half of the year the price had increased to £1.25 per metre. Of the 10,000 metres purchased, Dovetails still had 2,000 metres in stock unused at the end of the year. How should the 2,000 metres be valued?

Frame 10

	Note	19X1	19X0
		£	£
Current Assets			
Stocks	12	435,289	404,095

Note 12		
	£	£
Stocks		
Raw materials	211,579	195,026
Work in progress	202,993	187,792
Finished goods	20,717	21,277
	435,289	404,095

Accounting policies
(b) Stocks
Stocks and work in progress are stated at the lower of cost and net realisable value. Cost of materials is determined on a first in first out basis. For work in progress and finished goods, cost includes materials, direct labour and attributable production overheads. Net realisable value is based on estimated sales proceeds after allowing for all further costs of disposal and conversion of goods to their finished condition.

Dovetails might reasonably proceed on the basis that it will carry its earlier costs forward. In that case, the stock of unused timber at the end of the year would be valued at 95p per metre and would be included in the balance sheet at a value of £1,900. As a result, the profit and loss account would be charged with £9,100 (total cost of timber purchased £11,000, less value of stock carried forward £1,900).

Alternatively, Dovetails might choose to attach the earlier costs to the goods sold during the year and to carry forward the later costs. In that case the year-end stock of timber would be valued at £1.25 per metre and would be included in the balance sheet at a value of £2,500, and £8,500 would be charged against the current year's sales. The effect of the two alternative bases of valuation is to produce a cost of sales (and therefore a profit) figure which is different by £600 and a stock figure which is different by the same amount – a difference which in this example amounts to some 30 per cent of the balance sheet carrying value.

Frame 11 summarises the effect. The difference produced by the alternative bases (£600) arises from only one small element in Dovetails' total stocks of

£435,289. If costs had changed similarly during the year on all Dovetails' categories of stock, the magnified effect on the total balance sheet value could be as much as plus or minus £150,000 – more than Dovetails' total profit for the year!

Frame 11

Bases of stock valuation	Balance sheet	Profit and loss account
	Asset	Cost of sales
	£	£
A 2,000 metres at 95p	1,900	
3,000 metres at 95p + 5,000 metres at £1.25		9,100
B 2,000 metres at £1.25	2,500	
5,000 metres at 95p + 3,000 metres at £1.25		8,500

Basis B produces profits and stock values which are both £600 greater than those resulting from basis A.

It should be noted that the attempt to allocate costs between materials that have been consumed and those that remain on hand at the end of the year is not necessarily related to the physical flow of those materials through the business: the alternative assumptions which might be made – and the alternative methods of valuation they lead to – arise only as a result of the need to prepare accounts, and the consequent requirement to allocate costs between different accounting periods. Dovetails' accounting policy note on stock says that the cost of materials is determined on a 'first in first out' basis, which means that earlier costs are attributed to the cost of goods sold during the year and therefore that it is later costs which are used in the valuation of stock on hand at the end of the year – a method equivalent to basis B in the example in Frame 11.

The allocation of material costs is only one of the problems associated with stock valuations. Dovetails' accounting policy on stocks – which purports to describe the bases adopted in valuing it – states that 'cost' comprises not only the cost of materials but also 'direct labour and attributable production overheads'. This means that the costs at which work-in-progress and finished goods are shown include an allocation of the wages and other expenses that have been incurred in bringing that stock to its present state. Establishing precisely which expenses – and what proportion of them – are directly attributable to stock on hand is a matter requiring judgement and estimation.

For example, it is reasonably clear that the wages of a saw-bench operator for a year could with justification be allocated over the number of lengths of timber sawn up during the year or the number of pieces of furniture produced; and it would be a reasonable allocation of his wages if the amount that was deemed to be attributable to stock on hand at the end of the year was in the same proportion as the quantity of that stock to the total amount produced during the year. However, not all wages are that easily identified directly with production: the factory could not run if it were not supervised or maintained, but it is a matter for debate whether a proportion of the wages of the foremen or cleaners can be said to be directly attributable to the production of closing stock, or whether the whole amount of those costs should be written off on a time basis, as soon as they are incurred. Similar decisions have to be made in respect of the myriad other costs that fall under the heading of 'overheads'. Those decisions will have an immediate effect on both the amount at which stock is stated in the balance sheet and on the amount of profit that is reported for the year.

A third matter to be considered in the valuation of stocks is concerned with the occasions on which it is necessary to show them at a value which is less than cost. This point is also alluded to in Dovetails' accounting policy note, where it is disclosed that stocks and work-in-progress are stated 'at the lower of cost and net realisable value'. This is the prudence concept at work. There will be a number of reasons why the full costs included in stock may not be recoverable on eventual sale. Materials may have been damaged, or finished goods may have proven faulty, or the items in stock may comprise a line which has now gone totally out of fashion. For any of these reasons, stocks will be reduced to the amount, if any, which might reasonably be expected to be recovered from their eventual sale. That amount will be uncertain, and can often only be estimated within wide margins. These matters provide further cause for reflecting that the amount appearing against stock in a balance sheet is very much less than a precisely calculated figure.

Despite the potential variables in the methods of establishing a stock valuation, it should be noted that whatever assumptions are made, and whatever methods are adopted, there is a general requirement that they should be applied consistently from year to year.

Unless a change of treatment is announced prominently in the accounts, it can be assumed that if Dovetails, for example, based their stock valuation on latest raw material costs and exclude indirect factory overheads, then those are the procedures which they have followed and will follow from year to year. Despite a variety of possible valuation methods, the requirement for consistency ensures that, year on year, the adopted treatment should have no significant effect on reported profits. Over the life of a business, profits will always be the same: it is only by virtue of preparing annual accounts, and the need to value stocks at the end of each period, that the accounting policies adopted in that valuation can, if not applied consistently, have the effect of shifting profits from one year to another.

DEBTORS

Debtors represent the amounts due to Dovetails from customers to whom they have sold goods on credit terms. Dovetails' debtors have increased substantially over the previous year (see Frame 12). That could mean that customers are taking much longer to pay, or it could mean that the volume of sales and number of customers has increased. Once again the figure is not to be read in isolation.

Frame 12

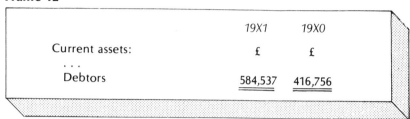

		19X1	19X0
Current assets:		£	£
. . .			
Debtors		584,537	416,756

For the most part, the debtors figure in a balance sheet emerges directly from the accounting records, and is one which is therefore capable of precise calculation. From their supporting records, Dovetails could identify how much of the total of £584,537 was due from each individual customer. The only degree of estimation involved concerns an assessment of whether any debtors will not be able to pay. Where there is evidence of bad or doubtful debts – and this will usually come from knowledge of the financial circumstances of the customers, and depending on how long the debts have been outstanding – prudence requires that they should be written down or provided for.

A provision for such debts (writing down the value of the asset debtors, and recognising an expense or loss in the profit and loss account) can be either 'specific' to the debts in question, or 'general' – in which case it is usually expressed as a percentage of sales or of outstanding debtors, and is based on previous years' experience of the proportion that ultimately are irrecoverable. Either way there are clearly elements of uncertainty and estimation involved in the calculation of the provision, and therefore in the amount at which debtors are stated in the balance sheet.

PREPAYMENTS

Conventionally, the amount shown for debtors will include any 'prepayments' made by the company. Prepayments represent the amounts of any expenses which have been paid for this year but which are attributable to succeeding years. Although these payments are already reflected in the accounting records, the matching principle requires that, on the preparation of accounts, adjustments should be made to carry forward as an asset that amount which should properly be recognised as an expense of the following year.

The degree of estimation involved in calculating the amount to be carried forward will depend on the type of expense in question. Where it is clearly identifiable with time periods, e.g. rent, the calculation is straightforward. Where it is not, e.g. advertising expenditure or costs in connection with the development of a new product, the estimate may involve a considerable degree of uncertainty. Where the amounts involved are significant, prepayments should usually be identified separately in the balance sheet. Where they are not shown separately it can usually be taken that they will represent only a small proportion of the figure appearing against debtors.

CASH

Almost alone amongst the items appearing in a balance sheet, cash is what it appears to be: the amount of cash on the premises or in the bank at 31 December 19X1 (see Frame 13). Even here, however, the incidence of uncleared cheques (those which have been issued, and recorded in the company's own records, but which have not yet been cleared through the bank statement) leaves room for some debate as to which is the correct figure to use – the one according to the cash book or the one according to the bank statement. Usual practice in the UK is to take the former – and to deduct uncleared cheque payments before disclosing both the bank balance and the amount of outstanding creditors.

Frame 13

	19X1	19X0
Current assets:	£	£
. . .		
Cash	26,333	29,745

Dovetails have some £3,000 less cash than they held a year ago, but that is not a figure that should be read in isolation, for as we shall see lower down in the balance sheet they also have a bank overdraft.

CURRENT LIABILITIES

In the same way as assets are distinguished in a balance sheet between fixed and current, the liabilities of a business are also grouped together according to whether they are payable in the short term or long term. Current liabilities are those amounts owed by the business which, in general, will fall due for payment within twelve months of the balance sheet date. For statutory reasons, the caption which groups them in the balance sheet is described as 'Creditors: amounts falling due within one year'.

In the supporting Note 13, Dovetails show four types of current liability: bank overdraft, trade creditors, taxation and dividend. Some of these will have to be paid in a matter of weeks: others may not fall due for several months. Nevertheless, grouping these various liabilities together under the one heading provides a neat and useful means of presenting an important part of the financial position of a business at a given date.

BANK OVERDRAFT

It was noted under current assets that Dovetails had cash and bank balances totalling £26,333. The accounts now show (see Frame 14) that they also have an overdraft – money owing to the bank – which at 31 December 19X1 amounts to £111,966

Frame 14

Note 13 Creditors: Amounts falling due within one year	19X1	19X0
	£	£
. . .		
Bank overdraft	111,966	85,599

The bank overdraft is secured by a fixed charge on the freehold property of the company.

When a bank grants an overdraft facility, it will usually be made available for a given period of time – often one year and, in normal circumstances, on the understanding that it will be available on a recurring basis thereafter. However, the terms under which it is lent will usually stipulate that an overdraft is repayable on demand; for this reason it is properly regarded as a current liability, even though there is an element of permanence to its recurring availability.

Note 13 reveals that the bank has taken a charge on the company's freehold property as security against the overdraft. If Dovetails defaults in repayment, the charge gives the bank the legal right to sell the property and recover the amount due to them out of the proceeds.

TRADE CREDITORS

Trade Creditors represent amounts owing to suppliers for goods and services provided to the company which have not yet been paid for. Dovetails owes amounts totalling £461,958 at 31 December 19X1, and owed a total of £329,877 at 31 December 19X0 (see Frame 15). In their accounting records, Dovetails will carry details of the amount it owes to each individual supplier and, as was the case with debtors, the amount of trade creditors is a liability which can be calculated quite accurately.

Frame 15

Note 13 Creditors: Amounts falling due within one year	19X1	19X0
	£	£
. . .		
Trade Creditors	461,958	329,877

Although no breakdown is given, creditors may also usually include any 'accrued' expenses. Accrued expenses arise from services that have been provided in the current year – the benefit of which has been used in earning the current year's revenue – but which have not been paid for until the following year. Thus at any given time – including the balance sheet date – money will usually be owing for the recent week's wages, in respect of interest due to the bank, or for the last quarter's electricity or telephone bill. In some cases the amounts owing will have to be estimated in advance of knowing their precise amount although, where the expenses in question are of a recurring nature, that estimate can be made with reasonable accuracy based on past experience of the annual, quarterly or monthly charge. Where accruals or other non-trade creditors are material in amount, the Companies Act requires them to be disclosed separately.

Although there are none in Dovetails' case, 'Current liabilities' may also include provisions for costs which although not yet paid, and even though no benefit may yet have been derived from them, are nevertheless 'provided for' this year on the basis of prudence. This will often be the case, for example, where – either through damage or negligence – machinery breaks down, or buildings fall into disrepair, and it is known that the assets in question can only be restored to their operating level at significant cost. Prudence requires provision for all known losses, even though these provisions can often only be made in round-sum amounts. Thus the pursuit of prudence adds another layer of estimation to the measurements included in accounts. Where any such provisions are made, company law requires them to be disclosed separately on the face of the balance sheet.

TAXATION

The next in Dovetails' list of creditors is taxation (see Frame 16), which amounted to £46,061 at 31 December 19X1 and £16,831 at 31 December 19X0. Companies pay corporation tax on their taxable profits. For most companies tax is usually payable nine months after the year end, and the amount of £46,061 is the estimated tax that Dovetails will have to pay for 19X1.

Frame 16

Note 13 Creditors: Amounts falling due within one year . . .	19X1 £	19X0 £
Taxation	46,061	16,831

DIVIDENDS

Dovetails' remaining creditor (see Frame 17) is described as a dividend of £21,600. A dividend is an amount paid out to the shareholders (the owners) of the company as a return on the funds they have invested by way of share capital.

It was established in Part One that profits accrue to capital. If a business makes profits, the shareholders' capital grows. They will be happy with that growth for it increases the paper value of their shares but, from time to time, they will also want a more tangible return on their investment. The only way that can normally be provided is by paying them a cash dividend.

Frame 17

Note 13	19X1	19X0
Creditors: Amounts falling due within one year	£	£
. . .		
Dividend	21,600	20,400

The amount of dividend the directors of a company decide to pay is a critical factor in their overall financial policy: as much as profit is distributed to shareholders, that much less profit is retained within the business to finance future growth. For companies listed on the Stock Exchange the pressure to 'maintain (or increase) the dividend' from year to year can be severe; indeed the amount of dividend can act as the primary influence on the price at which shares are quoted, and directors may often feel obliged to maintain dividend payments simply in the – sometimes erroneous – belief that that will keep up the share price, even though the company cannot really withstand the outflow of cash (which might then have to be borrowed elsewhere at high interest rates).

For some family companies the dividend decision will often be less critical. The shareholders are likely to be related, and some of them will usually have a direct interest in the day-by-day running of the company. They will therefore be just as concerned with the long-term growth of the business as they are with any short-term return on their investment.

Note that of the total amount of dividend that the directors of Dovetails have declared during the year the amount shown in the balance sheet represents only that part which remains unpaid at the end of the year. The full dividend story can only be obtained from the profit and loss account.

When a company makes a distribution, it is required to pay tax at the basic income tax rate on the gross, i.e. before tax, amount distributed. This amount is treated as a payment on account of the company's corporation tax liability for the year in which the dividend is paid. It is described as Advance Corporation Tax (ACT) and, in so far as it is recoverable, is treated as an asset in the balance sheet, usually by way of deduction from the deferred tax liability. Dovetails' dividend liability of £21,600 represents the net amount payable to shareholders after deducting tax.

NET CURRENT ASSETS

We have now almost walked through the first half of Dovetails' balance sheet. The next figure we meet is the amount of £404,574 which is described as 'net current assets'. It is arrived at by deducting total current liabilities of £641,585 from total current assets of £1,046,159.

The amount of net current assets is a critical figure in any balance sheet. It comprises one measure of the 'working capital' of the business and it is in order to be able to highlight this figure that current liabilities are presented as a deduction from current assets. Current liabilities are described as amounts which will fall due for payment within one year.

Current assets have been described as those amounts which are either already in the form of cash or will be turned into cash within one year. It is clear, therefore, that current assets will hopefully provide the funds from which current liabilities will be paid: the comparison of the two provides a useful indication of the short-term financial stability of the business.

Careful control of working capital lies at the heart of efficient business performance. It will form an important part of the analysis of Dovetails' financial strength and profitability, as described in Part Three.

LONG-TERM LOANS

Given the earlier definition of current liabilities, long-term liabilities will comprise amounts owed by the company which are repayable in more than a year's time; therefore the statutory caption 'Creditors: amounts falling due after more than one year'.

Note 14 in Dovetails' accounts (see Frame 18) explains that the company has borrowed £140,000 on which it has to pay a fixed rate of interest at 9 per cent per annum. The lenders have not been provided with any security for their loan. The note goes on to say that the loan is repayable at the company's discretion sometime between 2001 and 2005, but not later than 31 December 2005.

Frame 18

Note 14	*19X1*	*19X0*
	£	£
Long-term loan	140,000	140,000

The loan is unsecured, carries interest at 9% and is repayable at the company's option between 2001 and 2005, with a final redemption date of 31 December 2005.

Long-term loans of this sort can take a variety of forms. In Dovetails' case, the loan will be supported by a simple document issued to the lender in acknowledgement of the debt due to him. Alternatively, these loans can take the form of debentures, which is really no more than a different way of describing the piece of paper that acknowledges the debt. They can be secured (implying that the lenders have taken a charge over some of the company's assets as security for their debt), or unsecured. They are sometimes described as convertible, which means that at some time in the future the lender has the right to convert them into Ordinary shares in the company. They can be either redeemable, as with Dovetails, or irredeemable – in which case the company has no obligation to repay them (except in liquidation). There may even be a premium payable on final redemption, i.e. repayment, by the company. Their one essential characteristic is that they will usually carry a fixed rate of interest.

There are similarities here with preference shares. Preference shares will also carry a fixed return and they can be issued under terms which describe them as convertible or non-convertible, redeemable (at par or at a premium) or irredeemable. The critical difference is that interest on borrowings is an annual commitment which has to be met each year, regardless of whether the company has made any profits and before any of the shareholders – preference or otherwise – become entitled to any dividends. Interest is an expense which has to be paid and accounted for before calculating profit. Dividends to shareholders are dependent upon profitability.

The distinction between debt and equity capital is an important one. Each can provide a source of long-term finance for the company. From the point of view of the lender or the investor, the choice between a fixed rate of return or a return linked to profitability will depend very largely on the degree of risk inherent in the company's operations.

The same assessment of risks will also affect the choice from the company's point of view. Any preference for debt as a source of finance will depend very much on the required rate of interest. But it will also depend on the expected pattern of profitability. If profits are consistent from year to year, debt can provide an attractive source of long-term funds. If profits are volatile, the annual interest burden of debt could, in unprofitable years, prove terminal. For these reasons most companies will seek to achieve a careful balance between the two and it is this balance which is referred to as a company's 'gearing'. The choice between debt and equity lies at the heart of a company's long-term financing policy and an assessment of its gearing plays an important part in any examination of a company's financial stability. This matter is re-examined as a feature of the analysis in Part Three.

DEFERRED TAXATION

During the review of Dovetails' current liabilities it was observed that the amount appearing against taxation represented corporation tax payable on the taxable profit for the year. The amount of the tax charge, however, is rarely the result of a straightforward calculation between the profit shown in the accounts and the appropriate rate of corporation tax. Differences will usually arise because the rules by which the Inland Revenue calculate 'taxable profit' differ in certain respects from the principles that apply in the measurement of accounting profit.

The major difference concerns the capital allowances which are granted in respect of fixed assets. The accounting treatment of fixed assets is to depreciate them over their useful lives, resulting in an annual charge for depreciation in the profit and loss account. For tax purposes, however, the proportion of the cost of plant and machinery which is allowed as a deduction against profits (the rate of capital allowances) is governed by tax statute. Thus in computing the amount of profits on which tax is payable, the amount of any depreciation has to be added back to the profit shown in the accounts and the appropriate rate of capital allowance deducted.

At the time of writing capital allowances are granted on most types of plant and machinery at the rate of 25%. In recent years, however, they have been as much as 100% and at these levels the difference between the depreciation charge add-back and the capital allowance deduction can create very significant variations between accounting and taxable profit.

In order to illustrate the point, consider a machine which costs £1,000 and is depreciated over 10 years. Assume, for the purposes of this example, that the rate of corporate tax is 40% and that 100% capital allowances are available on the machinery in question. In Year 1, the depreciation charge in the accounts would be £100, whereas the deduction allowed for tax purposes will be the full cost of £1,000. As a result, the tax bill for the year will be less than it would otherwise have been by an amount of $40\% \times$ £900. In each of the nine subsequent years, the tax bill will be more (by an amount of $40\% \times £100$) than a straight 40% on the profit for the year. The incidence of capital allowances, therefore, is not to reduce the amount of tax payable in the long run but merely to defer its payment to later years. It is in order to retain the relationship between profits shown in the accounts and the full amount of tax payable in respect of those profits that it has become standard practice to provide not only for the amount of tax immediately payable but also for any tax in respect of those profits the payment of which has been deferred.

The principle is the same even with capital allowances standing at lower rates, such as the 25% currently available. The difference is one of degree: the closer the rate of capital allowances is to the rate of depreciation used in the accounts, so the amount of deferred tax which needs to be provided reduces.

Because the general trend has been to reduce the rate of capital allowances the general impact of deferred tax on companies' accounts is now less than it has been in recent years. Nevertheless, the need to provide for deferred tax is clear, if we consider it only in terms of a single piece of plant or machinery. The habit of most companies, however, is to replace their fixed assets from year to year as part of a continuous programme. In the earlier example we assumed that the company did not buy any further fixed assets after Year 1. If it had bought more plant in Year 2, further capital allowances would then have been available, and that year would therefore have been one of tax advantage rather than disadvantage. The same would apply to any plant that was acquired – and any allowance that was thereby obtained – in Years 3 and 4 and 5, and onwards. In each year there would be a tax advantage as long as the amount of capital allowances available exceeded the total amount of depreciation that was disallowed. To this extent an element of tax is deferred not temporarily but permanently. The permanence of the deferral will depend on the company's future capital investment programme: if the plans are for a steady, annual re-investment in fixed assets, there is the prospect of the attributable taxation not merely being deferred but never becoming payable at all. And this raises the question of whether it really needs to be provided for in the first place.

The assessment of future tax liabilities is a matter of some concern for accountants. In recent years there have been a number of different attempts at establishing standard accounting practice in this area. The latest version requires that provision should be made for all deferred taxation, except where it is unlikely that any liability will arise in the 'foreseeable future'. We might well ponder how much of the future is foreseeable and therefore question the practicalities of this standard treatment. Nevertheless, it is the one adopted by Dovetails, as described in their accounting policy.

Dovetails have estimated that in addition to the amount of tax that will be payable within nine months of the year end (and shown under current liabilities), there will be a probable further liability to taxation amounting to £99,107 (see Frame 19). [The net amount of £99,107 is made up of future estimated liabilities (arising from accelerated capital allowances) of £108,364, less recoverable ACT of £9,257.] That is really no more than the best guess that can be made at the end of December 19X1 of the proportion of the full potential liability (£147,500) which is likely to crystallise. The amount that will eventually prove to be payable over the next few years will depend on Dovetails' future capital expenditure programme; and it really cannot be said whether any amount that might fall due will be payable in two years' or in ten years' time.

Companies vary widely in their attitudes to deferred tax, and the uncertainty that surrounds any future liability – whether or not it is provided for in the accounts – is a matter which can cause some difficulty when it comes to assessing a particular company's financial position. The policy on deferred tax can also have a profound effect on the profit and loss account, where the extent to which it is or is not provided will have a direct and immediate impact on the amount of profits that are reported to be available for distribution to shareholders.

Frame 19

	19X1	19X0
	£	£
PROVISIONS FOR LIABILITIES AND CHARGES		
Deferred taxation	99,107	94,900

Note 15 Deferred taxation	£
At 1 January 19X1	94,900
Transfer from profit and loss account	4,721
Adjustment to advance corporation tax	(514)
At 31 December 19X1	99,107

	Amounts provided	
	19X1	19X0
	£	£
Accelerated capital allowances	108,364	103,643
Advance corporate tax	(9,257)	(8,743)
	99,107	94,900

If full provision were made, the potential liability would be as follows:		
Accelerated capital allowances	147,500	138,000

Accounting policies
(c) Taxation
The charge for taxation is based on the profit for the year, and takes into account taxation deferred because of timing differences in the treatment of certain items for accounting and taxation purposes, but only where there is reasonable probability of payment.

SHARE CAPITAL

In the case of a company, capital is divided into shares, each representing a stake in the ownership. Company law permits shares to be issued in various types, and in unlimited amount. The type and amount of shares issued by any one company, however, will be governed by its constituting documents (its Memorandum and Articles of Association). As well as representing an interest in the capital of the business, a share will usually carry with it the right to vote – on those occasions when shareholders are asked to decide on some important aspect of the company's affairs – as well as an entitlement to dividends and a share in the proceeds in the event of the company being liquidated.

Dovetails' balance sheet shows share capital of £120,000 (see Frame 20). Note 16 explains that this is made up of Ordinary shares of £1 each. The amount of £1 is the nominal or par value of each share, and it represents the minimum amount that would have been paid in when the shares were first issued. Ordinary shares are the type most commonly issued. Each will usually carry an equal right to vote, an equal right to any profits that are distributed and equal rights in the winding up of the company. The 'authorised' share capital is the maximum amount which the company is presently permitted to issue, although by altering its Memorandum, and on application to the Registrar of Companies, this amount can be increased.

Frame 20

	Note	19X1	19X0
		£	£
Called-up Share capital	16	120,000	120,000
Note 16			
Share capital			
Authorised:			
150,000 Ordinary shares of £1 each		150,000	150,000
Allotted and fully paid:			
120,000 Ordinary shares of £1 each		120,000	120,000

Of the 150,000 shares Dovetails has been authorised to issue, Note 16 confirms that it has in fact issued only 120,000.

The holders of Ordinary shares are not guaranteed any dividend. When profits are low they may get no return at all. When profits are high, however, they can usually expect a correspondingly high return on their investment. The strength of entitlement to dividends is the characteristic which distinguishes them from 'preference' shares. Dovetails do not have any preference shares in issue but, where they exist, they carry – as their name implies – preferred rights to any dividends that might be payable and any distributions that might be made on liquidation. Preference shares usually attract a fixed percentage return, which has to be satisfied before any dividend can be paid to the Ordinary shareholders. They therefore carry less risk than Ordinary shares and as a result will often be issued without voting rights. It is the Ordinary shareholders who provide the risk capital of the company and it is they who will reap the rewards if the company is successful.

RESERVES

The 'Reserves' caption in the balance sheet will often contain a number of quite separate balances. Dovetails' balance sheet, and the supporting Note 17 (see Frame 21), shows that their reserves contain two distinct elements: a share premium account amounting to £243,336 and revenue reserves which, at 31 December 19X1, totalled £316,192. These two amounts are quite different in their characteristics.

The share premium account represents money paid in by shareholders over and above the nominal value of the shares that they hold. The existence of a

Frame 21

	Note	19X1 £	19X0 £
Capital and Reserves			
Share premium account	17	243,336	243,336
Profit and loss account	17	316,192	276,037

Note 17 Reserves

	Share Premium £	Profit and loss account £
At 1 January 19X1	243,336	276,037
Retained profit	–	40,155
At 31 December 19X1	243,336	316,192

share premium account indicates that at some stage in the company's past a block of shares has been issued at a price in excess of their nominal value.

One of the primary functions of company law is to provide protection for the interests of creditors and other third parties who might enter into financial dealings with the company. One of the ways in which the law can do this is to provide safeguards to ensure that the capital subscribed by the shareholders is not subsequently and wilfully reduced, impaired or otherwise repaid to them – by way of dividend or otherwise – except in specified circumstances. Because it represents money subscribed by the shareholders, the same legal safeguards apply to the share premium account. The essential characteristic of a share premium account is, therefore, that it is non-distributable.

In that respect it is totally different from revenue reserves, which are fully distributable. Revenue reserves are sometimes alternatively described as retained profits. They represent the accumulation of profits made by a company during its lifetime, subject to the extent to which in the past those profits have been distributed by way of dividend. Thus a company which in its first year makes profits of £10,000, and pays a dividend of £2,000, will have revenue reserves or retained profits at the end of that year amounting to £8,000. If in the second year it makes profits of £12,000, and pays a dividend of £3,000, its revenue reserves at the end of Year 2 will amount to £17,000.

Dovetails' revenue reserves at the beginning of 19X1 amounted to £276,037. Of the profit made during 19X1, £40,155 was retained, leaving accumulated retained profits at 31 December 19X1 of £316,192.

It is important to recognise that the full amount of retained profits shown in a balance sheet is not necessarily immediately available for distribution to shareholders. A dividend can only be paid out of profits, but the dividend decision will depend just as much on whether there is sufficient cash available to pay it. It is rare that the full amount of a company's retained profits will be available in the form of cash. The purpose of retaining profits will usually have been to finance the further growth of the company, and those profits will usually have been re-invested or 'ploughed back' into other assets. Past profitability does not necessarily go hand in hand with present liquidity. To assess the amount of retained profits that are potentially available for distribution, we need to look also at the assets side of the balance sheet to see how much cash the company has available.

Although it does not figure in Dovetails' accounts, a third source of reserves will often arise as the result of a revaluation of assets. By way of exception to the general principle of historic cost, it is increasingly becoming the case that companies will obtain independent professional revaluations of certain of their assets (particularly property) which will then be included in their accounts at the higher revalued amount. In so far as profit, in its broadest sense, results from increases in net asset values, the surplus that arises on the revaluation of property can be regarded as a profit, and can therefore properly be regarded as part of the company's reserves. The essential difference, of course, is that as long as the company continues to use the property and does not sell it, that profit remains unrealised, and is therefore not distributable.

SUMMARY

We have now completed our 'walk through' Dovetails' balance sheet at 31 December 19X1. Before concluding, we might revert to the description of the balance sheet that was used in Part One and summarise where Dovetails now stands (see Frame 22).

At the end of 19X1 Dovetails has funds totalling £918,635. Of that amount, £679,528 came from capital introduced by the shareholders and from profits retained within the business; £239,107 has been borrowed long term.

Of the total funds available, £488,061 is invested in fixed assets and £26,000 in investments; £404,574 has been used to finance the company's working capital.

Dovetails' gross current assets have been financed as to £641,585 by short-term liabilities. To support the level of stock, debtors and cash they need to carry, totalling £1,046,159, Dovetails have 'borrowed' money from trade creditors, from the bank, from the tax authorities and, to the extent that they have not yet paid the dividend due to them, from shareholders.

Frame 22

Dovetails Limited

| Where does the business stand at the end of 19X1? |

| Where is the money now? |

	£	£
Fixed assets		488,061
Investments		26,000
Current assets	1,046,159	
Current liabilities	641,585	
(Working capital)		404,574
		918,635

| Where did it come from? |

		£
Capital and reserves		679,528
Long term liabilities		239,107
		918,635

5   The profit and loss account

If the balance sheet attempts to answer the financial question 'Where does the business stand?', the profit and loss account seeks to explain 'How well has the business done?'. Its function is to compare all the revenues earned by selling goods with all the expenses that have been incurred in earning them. This comparison will show whether the company has made a profit or a loss on trading. Note that whereas the balance sheet describes the financial position on a particular day, the profit and loss account summarises the results of trading over a given period, usually one year.

It has been established that all costs have to be described either as assets in the balance sheet or as expenses in the profit and loss account. Their inclusion in the balance sheet as an asset will depend on whether there is any benefit to be derived from them in future periods. It has also been established that the amount at which certain assets are stated in the balance sheet will often be a matter requiring a good deal of estimation, and it will now be clear that the converse effect of those estimates is reflected in the amount of expense that is recorded in the profit and loss account. It is also clear that the expenses that have to be incurred in the earning of revenue are great in their number and variety, including all the costs of converting raw materials into finished goods, as well as the costs of selling them, and the whole range of administration expenses that arise in the general course of running a business.

In its published form, the profit and loss account is a somewhat condensed statement, giving only a brief answer to the question 'How well did the business do?'. A limited amount of supporting information is given in the notes – particularly notes 2 and 3 to the accounts – but it is highly selective. By its nature (How much did the directors pay themselves? How much did the audit cost?) it can be seen to be the sort of information that is required to be disclosed by law. For the most part, it arises from the function which accounts serve in reporting to shareholders on how the directors have conducted their stewardship of the company's affairs.

As far as the businessman is concerned, the published form of profit and loss account tells him little about how well he did and even less about why he did not do better. If the businessman wants to use his accounts to plan and control his business, he will need more detailed information than is given here. For the time being, however, we can examine the story as it is told by Dovetails' profit and loss account in its presently published form.

TURNOVER

The first line in Dovetails' profit and loss account shows turnover for 19X1 of £2,424,900 (see Frame 23). Turnover represents the total amount of revenue earned during the year from the company's normal trading

Frame 23

	19X1	19X0
	£	£
TURNOVER	2,424,900	1,993,400
Cost of sales	1,786,474	1,435,850
Gross profit	638,426	557,544

operations. In Dovetails' case, it would be made up of the total sales value (excluding VAT) of furniture delivered and invoiced to customers during 19X1. Note that Dovetails' turnover is greater this year than it was last. That could mean that the volume of their sales has increased, or it could mean that they have sold the same amount of furniture at higher prices.

DISCONTINUED OPERATIONS

Although it does not apply in Dovetails' case, a relatively recent accounting standard has introduced the requirement to disclose separately the revenues and costs attributable to any part of the business which has been discontinued. Where applicable, therefore, published profit and loss accounts will include columns which split turnover, costs and operating profit between continuing and discontinued operations. The purpose is to give investors and other readers of accounts better information on which to assess the likely future performance of a business.

GROSS PROFIT

The turnover figure is followed by a deduction in respect of cost of sales. In Dovetails' case these costs will represent the direct costs of making the furniture which is sold – primarily labour and materials. The resultant figure – gross profit – is one of the most important items in a set of accounts. It results from a direct comparison between what the product can be sold for and what it costs to make it, and the resultant 'margin' has to be sufficient to cover all the other costs and overheads involved in running the business.

Dovetails have made more gross profit in 19X1 (£638,426) than they did in 19X0 (£557,544), but that would be expected – they have made more sales in 19X1. The picture is much clearer if gross profit is expressed as a percentage of sales:

$$19X1 \quad \frac{638426}{2,424,900} \times 100 = 26.3\%$$

$$19X0 \quad \frac{557544}{1,993,400} \times 100 = 28.0\%$$

Now we can see that the gross margin on sales has in fact decreased from 28.0% in 19X0 to 26.3% in 19X1. A higher level of business has been achieved, but only at a lower margin. That may or may not have been a good thing, and behind this single gross margin statistic lies a whole range of critical business indicators: how well has the selling price been fixed; how closely have the costs of production been controlled; and, most importantly, whether the extra gross profit generated from higher sales, albeit at lower margin, has been sufficient to cover any increases in the other overheads of running the business at the higher level of activity. All these matters we shall return to in the analysis in Part Three.

OPERATING PROFIT

For the time being we can observe (Frame 24) that Dovetails' other costs (distribution, administration, other operating expenses) have increased by £82,589 (from £399,718 in 19X0 to £482,307 in 19X1), that the increase in gross profit has been insufficient to cover them, and that as a result the business has suffered an overall drop in net operating profit from £157,826 in 19X0 to £156,119 in 19X1.

Frame 24

	19X1 £	19X0 £
GROSS PROFIT	638,426	557,544
Distribution costs	98,637	72,005
Administration expenses	119,137	118,678
Other operating charged (net)	264,533	209,035
	482,307	399,718
OPERATING PROFIT	156,119	157,826

Operating profit is the key figure in the accounts. It represents the net result of trading for the year and is arrived at by comparing total sales revenue with total expenses incurred in earning that revenue. It represents the ultimate measure of whether it has been worthwhile staying in business. Dovetails has made a profit, but how good it is, how well the business has done, needs deeper analysis, and that analysis needs more information than is typically contained within published accounts. The additional information we need, and which the businessman needs in order to monitor his trading performance properly, is more typically found in the sort of management accounts which are included and analysed in Part Three

EXCEPTIONAL ITEMS

The next line in Dovetails' profit and loss account (see Frame 25) describes an exceptional item of £18,342. 'Exceptional' items are costs or revenues which, because of their size or nature, need to be separately disclosed for the accounts to show a true and fair view.

Frame 25

Note 8	19X1	19X0
	£	£
Exceptional Item	18,342	

Redundancy and other costs relating to the closure of the Scunthorpe factory (less related taxation of £19,012).

Past accounting practice used to distinguish between items which were 'extraordinary' and those which were 'exceptional'. Extraordinary items were distinguished by being derived from events which fell outside 'normal business activities'. The judgement of whether an event fell inside or outside normal business activities would often be difficult and subjective and the consequent impact on the reported results could be critical: extraordinary items were traditionally treated 'below the line' ie. *after* arriving at profit on ordinary activities.

Because of these difficulties of interpretation, and their potentially conflicting treatments, recent accounting standards have re-defined the scope of 'normal business activities' to the point where extraordinary items are now virtually extinct.

Note 7 explains that Dovetails' exceptional charge is in respect of redundancy and other costs connected with the closure of one of their factories. These costs are significant in the context of the company's overall results in both their amount and their nature, and therefore warrant separate disclosure.

The next line the profit and loss account is interest payable. Note 4 shows how the amount is made up.

Frame 26

Note 4	19X1	19X0
	£	£
Bank Interest	13,686	11,008
Interest on long-term loan	12,600	12,600
	25,386	23,608

The charge is shown as a separate item to distinguish costs incurred in using finance. Without this separate disclosure two businesses with the same trading profits could show different results, according to whether they use their own money (with no interest cost) or borrowed funds.

TAXATION

Most of what needs to be said about taxation has been covered in the discussion of the taxation amounts appearing in the balance sheet. As far as the profit and loss account is concerned (see Frame 25), it is notable that, on a trading profit of £129,833, Dovetails estimate that the corporation tax payable will amount to £49,736. Note 7 shows how this figure is broken down into the amount that is payable in the near future (and which will therefore be shown as a current liability) and the amount by which the liability is expected to be deferred.

DIVIDENDS

After accounting for taxation and extraordinary items, £61,755 of the profits Dovetails have made in 19X1 remain available for distribution to shareholders. Of this amount, Dovetails' directors have decided to distribute £21,600 and to retain £40,155 in the business. The 19X1 dividend amounts to a return of 18p on each of the 120,000 Ordinary shares of £1 each (see Frame 27): Note that Dovetails' dividend is bigger this year than it was last, even though last year's profits were higher.

Frame 27

Note 9	19X1	19X0
	£	£
Dividend	21,600	20,400
Note 9		
Dividend		
Proposed Ordinary dividend of		
18p (19X0 – 17p) per share	21,600	20,400

It is preferable – although not necessary – that the amount of dividend declared should be seen to be covered by the current year's profit. However dividends can also be paid out of profits which have been retained in earlier years, even if the current year has resulted in a trading loss. Dovetails' directors would be legally entitled to declare a dividend of up to £316,192 (the full amount of their retained revenue reserves at December 19X1). But this would be impossible in the short term (because the cash is not available) and would be a dubious policy even in the long term (because the company's net assets would be reduced by about half).

Dividend policy is therefore something which needs to be assessed in terms of both current and past profits, as well as in terms of current liquid resources and the requirements for the future. Of their profit for 19X1, Dovetails' directors are retaining £40,155 in the business. From their point of view, that retention will provide a further basis for the company's continuing growth. From the shareholders' point of view, that retention represents a growth of capital, an increase in the value of their interest in the business. The balance sheet shows the shareholders' interest to have increased from £639,373 to £679,528. The profit and loss account shows how that increase came about.

6   The Cash Flow Statement

The purpose of the cash flow statement – the third chapter in the story told by the accounts – is to explain how far the business has managed to generate cash during the year, where the cash has come from, and how it was used.

It should be noted that the information contained in the cash flow statement does not emerge directly from the accounting process in the same way as do the figures which appear in the balance sheet and profit and loss account. Indeed the function of the statement is to provide no more than further analysis and re-presentation of information which, for the most part, is already contained in the other two main statements.

That is not to say that the cash flow statement does not provide a further valuable insight into the operation of a business. Thus, a balance sheet will describe, at a given date, where the total funds presently available to a business have come from and how they are presently deployed; and a profit and loss account will show whether funds have been increased (a profit) or decreased (a loss) by the results of trading. The cash flow statement, however, explains the changes in financial strength and standing of the business that have arisen as the result not only of trading but also of any other major business transactions which have taken place during the year.

The particular value of the cash flow statement is that it focuses on the cash generated and absorbed by a business, and on the consequent improvement or deterioration in business liquidity.

There are six main headings to Dovetails' cashflow statement with three supporting notes which provide details on how certain of the figures have been derived. The sum of the six parts aggregates to the net increase or decrease in cash generated during the year.

The first heading is described as 'Net cash inflow from operating activities' and the figure is derived from the reconciliation shown in Note 18 (see Frame 28). This reconciliation is needed because accounts are prepared on the accruals basis and operating profit will therefore include items which do not necessarily involve the inflow or outflow of cash.

The first reconciling item is in respect of depreciation of £65404. The point here is that the charge for depreciation is an accounting adjustment: it did not give rise to a cash outflow. The outflows occurred when the related fixed assets were acquired and would be accounted for in the cashflow statement, in the year in which they were acquired, at their full costs of acquisition.

Frame 28

Note 18

Reconciliation of operating profit to net
cash inflow from operating activities

	£
Operating profit	156,119
Depreciation charges	65,404
Profit on sale of tangible fixed assets	(3,907)
Exceptional items	(18,342)
Increase in stocks	(31,194)
Increase in debtors	(167,781)
Increase in creditors	132,081
Net cash inflow from operating activities	132,380

The same reasoning applies to the adjustment which is made in Dovetails' note 18 for the profit on sale of fixed assets (£3,907)*. The inflow of funds that results from those disposals amounts not just to the profit but to the full amount of the proceeds. For the purposes of the statement, therefore, the profit on disposal is eliminated and the proceeds of £5,500* are included in full lower down in the statement.

Changes in the components of working capital during the year also result in an increase or decrease in cash funds. If stock held at the end of the year is greater than held at the beginning, more cash has been invested: ie a decrease in cash. Conversely, a rise in creditors results in an increase in cash as less has been paid over to suppliers: cash funds have been retained.

Taking these various adjustments into account, the reconciliation in Note 18 shows that Dovetails' operating profit of £156,119 converts into a net inflow on a cash basis of £132,380.

The second heading in the cashflow statement 'Returns on investments and servicing of finance', supported by Note 19, shows details of interest paid and received.

---

*The profit of £3,907 arises from a comparison of the net book value of the assets sold with the proceeds of selling them. Note 10, which describes movements on Dovetails' fixed assets, shows that during the year Dovetails disposed of assets which had originally cost £18,866 and on which the accumulated depreciation amounted to £17,273. Their net book value at the time of disposal was therefore £1,593 and, if the proceeds obtained from selling them resulted in a profit of £3,907, we can deduce that those proceeds must have amounted to £5,500.

Frame 29

Note 19

Returns on investments and
servicing of finance

	£
Interest received	–
Interest paid	26,286
	26,286

Here again, the figures represent amounts paid or received and may differ from corresponding amounts shown in the profit and loss account to the extent that these include any element of accrual.

Similarly with the next line in the statement 'Taxation'. The amount shown is the amount of tax that Dovetails paid during 19X1 and will usually represent payment of the tax provided for in the accounts of the previous year. Dovetails tax charge for 19X1, as provided in the profit and loss account, will figure in the cashflow statement for 19X2, assuming they pay it in 19X2.

The fourth part of Dovetails' cashflow statement, supported by Note 19, shows capital expenditure of £99,174.

Frame 30

Note 19

Capital expenditure

	£
payments to acquire tangible fixed assets	100,674
payments to acquire trade investments	4,000
receipts from sales of tangible fixed assets	(5,500)
	99,174

As discussed earlier, the amount spent on the acquisition of fixed assets represents their full cost and can be identified as 'additions' in Note 10 to the accounts. Receipts represent full proceeds on disposal.

The fifth heading shows 'Equity dividends paid'. Once again the cash basis applies. The dividend shown in Dovetails' profit and loss account, although provided for in 19X1, will not be paid until 19X2. The amount paid out in 19X1 is £20,400, the dividend relating to the prior year.

The sixth part of the statement is headed 'Financing'. Here, typically, would be included any cash raised from the issue of new shares or from loans or hire purchase or leasing arrangements. In Dovetails' cases there are none.

The resultant, key figure in the statement shows whether the net cash position of the business has improved or worsened as a result of the year's activities, the consequence of which is summarised in Note 20.

Frame 31

Note 20			
Analysis of changes	1 Jan 19X1	Cashflows	31 Dec 19X1
Cash	29,745	(3,412)	26,333
Bank overdraft	(85,559)	(26,367)	(111,966)
	(55,854)	(29,779)	(85,633)

Liquid funds are shown as the net aggregate of cash balances and bank overdraft. In Dovetails' case, largely as a result of their investment in fixed assets, net liquid resources have decreased by £29,779 during the year.

PART THREE

ANALYSIS OF ACCOUNTS: HOW TO USE THEM

7 Outline

The first two parts of this book have examined the content of accounts in terms of how they are made, i.e. the principles that are adopted in preparing them, and what they say, i.e. what the words mean and how the figures are arrived at. Part Three describes how accounts can be analysed and how careful analysis can provide valuable insights into the state of a business. In particular, we shall be concerned to examine how a businessman can use his accounts to:

Control the current performance of his business

Plan for improved performance in the future.

For the most part, the tools of analysis take the form of ratios and comparisons. There are of course a great number of ratios that can be extracted from a set of accounts. The following chapters concentrate only on the most important ones. Most are designed to help the businessman in managing his business, and can be conveniently grouped under the general heading of management ratios. Each is designed to address one of the two basic questions which lie at the heart of business performance:

Profitability – how well has the business done, and how might it do better?

Liquidity – what is its financial state of health, and how can it be made stronger?

In the case of medium-sized companies such as Dovetails, the businessman will often have an interest in his business not only as a manager but also as an investor. Under the general heading of proprietary ratios, later chapters therefore describe some of the ways in which business proprietors and shareholders generally can use their accounts to assess the value and security of their private investment.

8   Methods of analysis

USEABLE INFORMATION

Accounts provide a great deal of information. We can learn very quickly from reading Dovetails' accounts, for example, that the company made a profit of £129,833 in 19X1, or that it spent £100,674 on fixed assets, or that it had stocks of £435,289 at the end of the year . . . and so on. All that is informative, but it is not necessarily useful. Before we put the question 'How can that information be used?' we might first consider some of the factors which cause us to regard information in general as being useful or otherwise.

Consider the statement: 'A young man weighs 14 stone'. Of itself, it is difficult to know what to make of that piece of information. We might conclude differently according to whether we were told that he was 18 or 8 years old; and our assessment would vary according to whether he was 6 feet or 4 feet tall. We might take a more favourable view if we knew that twelve months ago he weighed 19 stone, whereas the same information would cause concern if his weight last year was 10 stone. And if we are to make any judgement of his condition, it would also be useful to know the average weight for men of his height and age.

So it is with accounts. Taken line by line, or item by item, individual pieces of information taken from accounts will be of limited value if they are read in isolation. If we are to make use of that information, we need to assess it against other pieces of related information. Identifying relationships between items in accounts and expressing that relationship in a useable form is the first step in unlocking the full potential value of accounting information.

RATIOS

Consider the statement included in a balance sheet that debtors at the end of the year amounted to, say, £1,000. Of itself, that is not a statement which can be used to any great purpose. We know, however, that debtors arise from sales. If sales for the year were also £1,000, the amount of outstanding debtors would be viewed with concern: the inference would be that no money had been collected from any customers throughout the year. If sales were £10,000, our view of debtors would be more favourable. Debtors would then represent only 10 per cent of sales for the year. The other 90 per cent would have been realised in cash, and that statistic clearly reflects better on the ability of the company to collect money from its customers.

COMPARISONS

We cannot say, however, whether that debtor/sales ratio is good or bad, better or worse than it might have been. To do that we need a point of reference by which to compare and assess it. There are three primary sources of comparison for accounting information.

If accounts show what has happened this year, the first useful point of comparison is with what happened last year. If, last year, debtors represented 12 per cent of sales then 10 per cent this year would indicate an improvement; if the debtors/sales ratio last year was 6 per cent, the position has worsened, indicating that the company's collection performance has deteriorated.

The assessment of trends is one of the most important uses which a businessman can make of his accounts. The accounts themselves provide comparative information for the previous year, but there is no reason why the assessment should be limited to two years. The longer the period over which a trend can be observed, the better the basis from which to predict its course in the future. Five years would certainly not be too long a period. If the pattern is improving, those features of business performance are to be developed and encouraged. If the trend is deteriorating, corrective action is needed. Either way, an assessment of the trend of past and present performance is a most valuable tool in charting the path to better performance in the future.

The second potential source of comparison is with budgets: to compare what has happened with what was expected to happen. A full discussion of standard-setting and the techniques of variance analysis falls outside the scope of this book. It should be noted, however, that the preparation of budgets is an important feature of business planning; and regularly monitoring actual against budgeted or expected performance is one of the most useful means by which management can exercise day-to-day control over the affairs of the business.

The third potential source of comparison is with similar businesses in the same industry. There are a number of publications that summarise and compare business performance in various sectors of industry. They do, however, derive the bulk of their information from larger public companies and the private businessman should take care not to compare his own performance too closely with others who might be operating in different conditions and under different circumstances. A better source of comparative statistics might be those available from the appropriate trade association.

A direct source of comparison – for companies – is from the accounts that are required to be put on public record. In the same way as the businessman uses his accounts to assess his own business performance, one of the best ways for him to evaluate that performance is by analysing the published accounts of his immediate competitors.

A final source – and one which is probably not tapped as much as it should be – is the use the businessman can make of his accountant who, in his professional capacity, will often act for a number of clients in the same trade. While his dealings with each will of course be confidential to the particular client, the professional accountant does, in the nature of his work, obtain a global view of trends within particular trades and his knowledge of average performance between a number of similar clients could provide a useful benchmark against which he can measure each result.

EVALUATION

Whatever the ratios, and whatever the means of comparison, a third and critical element in the use of accounts is the interpretation that is placed on the results of the analysis. Accounts can reveal what has happened, but not why. Ratios provide the tools, but to use them effectively the businessman needs to evaluate the movements and changes in them against his knowledge of the business and its trading circumstances.

If it was known that the young man, who had reduced his weight from 19 to 14 stone, had been dieting for the past 12 months, we would say that it was to be expected that he would lose weight. Similarly with business performance. If, for example, the price of timber has increased dramatically during the year, that factor would, on the face of it, be expected to affect the profitability of a furniture manufacturer. Similarly, a 5 per cent increase in sales might be interpreted as a creditable achievement in a declining market; less so in a buoyant one. Or if recent policy has been to offer substantial discounts to customers for prompt payment, an improvement in the ratio of debtors to sales would be expected, and would be a cause for investigation if it did not arise. It is against this sort of background knowledge of his business, the factors that have affected it and the circumstances in which it has had to trade, that the businessman should interpret the information which comes out of his accounts and evaluate his relative business performance.

One final point on the matter of interpretation: care should be taken not to place too much emphasis on any one ratio or percentage in isolation. A healthy increase in sales, for example, will usually be a good sign – but not if those increased sales have only been achieved at a price which offers little or no profit. Similarly, the offer of discounts for prompt payment might work to the advantage of cashflow, but it might also work to the disadvantage of business profitability.

SUMMARY

In summary, accounts can be used to plan and control business performance by:

- Identifying inter-relationships between individual items within the accounts, and expressing those relationships in the useable form of ratios or percentages.

- Comparing amounts or ratios for the current year
  a   with those for previous years, so as to establish trends;
  b   with budgets or expectations, to identify unusual or unexpected variations (or expected or anticipated variations which fail to occur);
  c   with similar businesses, to assess relative performance.

- Evaluating the results of this analysis against a background knowledge of the business, its recent policy, and the circumstances of trading .

- Taking appropriate action – to encourage favourable trends and correct unfavourable ones.

In this last respect, the action that is taken will of course depend to some extent on the wider business plan – whether, for example, the present objective is growth or survival; whether the present strategy is expansion or containment; whether the immediate need is for more profits, or a greater share of the market, or more ready cash. Whatever the policy, a careful analysis of accounts will reveal its success or failure, and will indicate those parts of the business or areas of activity to which management needs to direct its attention if the objectives are to be achieved.

These principles of analysis will now be applied to the accounts of Dovetails. Of necessity, the focus of comparison in these pages will be to assess the current year's performance against that for the previous year (rather than against budget, or that of other businesses). The purpose throughout, however, will be to address the two basic themes which lie at the heart of business performance: profitability and liquidity.

9 Analysis for business managers – profitability

PROFIT

How much profit did Dovetails make in 19X1? Their profit and loss account for the year shows four levels of profit:

	£
Profit before interest	137,777
Operating profit before tax	111,491
Profit for financial year	61,755
Retained profit	40,155

Each of these measures of profit will have their uses – according to the particular aspect of the business that is being assessed. The level of retained profit, for example, will indicate the extent to which management has sought to retain funds within the business to support its future growth. The figure for profit after tax and extraordinary items will be of particular interest to shareholders: it shows the amount of profit earned in the year which is available for dividends. For the purposes of assessing overall business performance, however, and particularly for the purpose of assessing relative performance year by year, the most appropriate indicator will be the amount of operating profit before tax.

PROFITABILITY

Dovetails' operating profit for 19X1 was £156,119 but, of itself, that does not provide a sufficient basis from which to assess the company's performance. It is the same with any form of income: if an investor had earned £1,000 in a year, we could not say whether he had done well or badly without knowing the amount he had invested: £1,000 earned on investments of £5,000 would be a better achievement than earning the same income from £50,000 of investments. Similarly with income generated by a business: two companies earning the same profit are not equally profitable if one has to use twice as much capital. In order to measure business performance, profits have to be related to the resources that are used in earning them: the information contained in the profit and loss account has to be related to that contained in the balance sheet.

CAPITAL EMPLOYED

In the same way as the profit and loss account gives several different levels of profit, so the balance sheet can give several readings for capital. For the purposes of assessing profitability, however, the measure of capital employed should reflect the full value of resources available to management during the year. All sources of capital should be included, whether loan or equity, and including the funds which are available as the result of retaining profits within the business.

Dovetails' balance sheet shows that the funds available at the start of the year totalled £874,273, and came from:

	£
Share capital	120,000
Retained profits and reserves	519,373
Long-term loan	140,000
Deferred taxation	94,900
	874,273

Viewed from the other side of the balance sheet, these funds were represented by:

		£
Fixed assets		454,384
Investments		22,000
Current assets	850,596	
Less: current liabilities	452,707	
		397,889
		874,273

Note that current liabilities are excluded from the calculation of capital employed. Although representing a source of finance, they are by definition only available on a short-term basis and they are, for the most part, closely identifiable with the current assets which they support. The amount of capital employed is therefore represented by the aggregate of fixed assets, investments, and the net investment in working capital (current assets less current liabilities).

These definitions should not be regarded as inviolable. The reference here for example has been to resources available at the *start* of the year: if Dovetails had received a substantial injection of new capital during 19X1, that fact should be taken into account (by averaging) when calculating the amount of capital employed. Similarly, there may be circumstances in which a bank overdraft is better regarded as a permanent source of long-term funds – and therefore as part of capital employed – rather than as a deduction from net working capital. The important point is that the figures for profit and capital employed should be extracted on a consistent basis.

RETURN ON CAPITAL EMPLOYED

Expressed in the form of a percentage, this relationship is usually referred to as the return on capital employed. It is the primary indicator of business performance. For Dovetails, the figures are as shown in Frame 32.

Frame 32

	19X1	19X0
	£	£
Operating profit	156,119	157,826
Capital employed	874,273	757,651*
Return on capital employed	17.9%	20.1%

Dovetails' achieved a return of 17.9 per cent in 19X1. It should be noted, however, before too much is read into that single statistic, that it is only as good as the figure on which it is based. Earlier discussion in this book has underlined the degree of estimation and judgement involved in preparing accounts. Thus a different method of stock valuation, or a different depreciation policy, would have produced different figures in both the profit and loss account and the balance sheet. They would have produced a different amount of profit and a different amount of capital employed – and would therefore have given the appearance of different profitability.

In particular, the principle of historic cost serves in times of inflation to understate the value of assets employed. A return of 17.9 per cent would show a dramatic decline if Dovetails had, for example, to replace their old plant and machinery (stated at old historic cost) with new equipment (stated at much higher replacement cost). The possible disparity between the age (and therefore the cost) of their fixed assets is one reason why comparisons between the returns on capital employed of two apparently similar businesses should only be made with care. For any one business, however, the principle of consistency ensures that accounts will be drawn up on a comparable basis from year to year, and the percentage return on capital employed will therefore provide a reliable basis for comparing relative profitability from one year to the next.

Dovetails have been less profitable in 19X1 (a return of 17.9 per cent) than they were in 19X0 (20.1 per cent). A first answer to the question 'How well did they do?' is therefore 'Not as well as last year'. Comparing these returns with those for the previous, say, five years would reveal whether the fall in 19X1 was exceptional or whether it represented a continuation of steadily declining trend.

*Representing the amount of capital employed at the start of 19X0. This figure is taken from Dovetails' previous balance sheet and is not readily available from the accounts reproduced in this book.

A second answer to the question 'How well did they do?' might come from comparing Dovetails' profitability with that of other similar businesses. That comparison would show whether Dovetails' experience was unusual or whether it was typical of the general decline in the industry.

Whatever the case, further analysis can indicate why the company has been less profitable, and where corrective action is needed.

ELEMENTS OF PROFITABILITY

Profits come from sales. Sales arise from the productive use of assets. The key to profitability is to recognise that it arises not only from the project margin on sales, but also from the effective use of capital.

The principle can be simplified by analogy. Jack and Jill both have identical capital of £20,000 represented by a villa in Spain. Each time they let their property, the rental income less the costs involved provides each of them with the same profit margin of £350 per month. Jack manages to let his for three months in the summer, and therefore makes a profit of £1,050 for the year – which represents a return of approximately 5 per cent. Jill lets hers for six months. Her return of 11 per cent is better not because she charges a higher rent but because she puts her villa to better use – she makes her capital work harder.

In the case of a business, profitability results from both

- The ability to generate profit from a given volume of sales; and

- The ability to generate sales from a given volume of capital.

The formula for return on capital employed can therefore be expressed as:

$$\frac{\text{Profit}}{\text{Capital employed}} = \frac{\text{Profit}}{\text{Sales}} \times \frac{\text{Sales}}{\text{Capital employed}}$$

Thus a 16 per cent overall return on capital employed might alternatively result, for example, from a profit margin on sales of 8 per cent multiplied by a ratio of sales to capital employed (referred to as turnover of capital employed) of 2, or from a profit to sales percentage of 1 multiplied by a capital turnover rate of 16. The first example would be more appropriate to heavy manufacturing industry. The second might be typical of supermarkets, who traditionally operate on low margins and high turnover. The figures which result from applying this analysis to Dovetails are summarised in Frame 33.

They show that the company's return on capital employed has fallen (from 20.1 to 17.9 per cent) despite a more efficient use of capital (the ratio of sales to capital employed has increased from 2.6 to 2.8). The main problem

Frame 33

	Return on capital employed	=	Profit / Sales	x	Sales / Capital
	£000s		£000s		£000s
19X1	$\dfrac{142}{874}$		$\dfrac{156}{2,424}$	x x	$\dfrac{2,424}{874}$
	17.9		6.4	x	2.8
19X0	$\dfrac{147}{758}$		$\dfrac{158}{1,993}$	x x	$\dfrac{1,993}{758}$
	20.5		7.9	x	2.6

appears to be that increased sales have not resulted in a proportionate increase in profit: the net profit percentage has fallen from 7.9 to 6.4 per cent. In other words, the company generated £2.8 worth of sales for every £1 of capital employed in 19X1 (whereas it only generated £2.6 in 19X0), but each £1 of sales generated only 6.4p of profit – compared with 7.9p in 19X0.

The sections that follow illustrate how the analysis of Dovetails' performance can be extended in more detail. It should be clearly established, however, that each step in the analysis flows from one or other of the twin roots of profitability: the margin on sales on the one hand and the efficient use of capital on the other.

PROFIT: SALES

There are two ways in which the ratio of profit to sales can be improved: increase selling prices or reduce costs. The first is a marketing decision and accounts cannot help – except by indicating how far past selling prices have or have not been sufficient to recover past costs. In the second respect – the control of costs – accounts provide not only a useful but an essential management tool.

CONTROLLING COSTS: GROSS PROFIT MARGINS

Costs can of course be analysed in a variety of different ways – by product, by department, by month – and costing records can be introduced into the accounting system according to the particular requirements of management.

So far in this book we have been concerned only with annual, financial accounts, and the point has already been made that in its published form the

Frame 34

DOVETAILS LIMITED

**Detailed profit and loss account
for the year ended 31 December 19X1**

	19X1 £	19X1 %	19X0 £	19X0 %
Sales	2,424,900	100	1,993,400	100
Cost of sales:				
Materials	1,335,217	55.1	1,105,190	55.4
Wages	451,257	18.6	330,666	16.6
	1,786,474	73.7	1,435,856	72.0
Gross profit	638,426	26.3	557,544	28.0
Overhead expenses:				
Production	264,533	10.9	209,035	10.5
Distribution	98,637	4.1	72,005	3.6
Administrative	119,137	4.9	118,678	6.0
	482,307	19.9	399,718	20.1
Net operating profit, before interest and taxation	156,119	6.4	157,826	7.9

annual profit and loss account is a document of limited usefulness: to pursue the analysis of profitability we need more information than it presently contains.

Frame 34 therefore reproduces Dovetails' profit and loss account with the addition of a little more detail. The more detailed statement shows how the various broad categories of costs have reduced sales of £2,424,900 in 19X1 to a profit of £156,119. The first half of the statement compares the revenue from goods sold during the year with the direct costs of producing those goods – in Dovetails' case the costs of timber and labour that go into the making of furniture. The second half of the statement summarises, by type of expenditure, the various overhead expenses that are incurred in running the business.

Comparisons with the previous year are made much easier if the figures are expressed in the form of percentages – in this case as a percentage of sales. Immediately the picture becomes clearer: the key percentages in Frame 34 show that for every £1 generated from sales, Dovetails spent:

	19X1, p	19X0, p
On materials	55.1	55.4
On wages	18.6	16.6
On overheads	19.9	20.1
Leaving, as profit	6.4	7.9
	100.00	100.00

Increased wage costs (from 16.6 to 18.6 per cent of sales) can now be seen to be the main cause of Dovetails' declining profitability. Management can investigate (if they do not already know) how far those increased costs are due to wage rate increases, or how far they are attributable to lower productivity. Whatever the cause, Dovetails have been unable to pass the full impact of the increased costs on to their customers: they have instead eroded profit margins, and actions will be needed to correct the trend of wage costs if they are not to erode those margins still further.

Increased wage costs have caused Dovetails' gross profit margin to fall from 28 to 26.3 per cent. In other respects, Dovetails have done well to restrict the fall in profits to this level. The average price of timber increased during 19X1 by some 4 per cent over the previous year. All other things being equal, a 4 per cent increase in material costs would, based on their 19X0 results, have wiped out 30 per cent of Dovetails' profit (4 per cent of £1,105,190 equals 28 per cent of £157,826). Clearly, the company has managed to pass on the bulk of this price increase to its customers. Alternatively they may have improved production methods, or reduced wastage. Their success may in part have been due to astute buying in anticipation of sharp price increase. One way or the other Dovetails have, against this sort of background, done well to limit their fall in profitability to the extent that they have.

CONTROLLING COSTS: OVERHEADS

The use of accounts to identify cost changes (and then to investigate and control them) can, of course, be extended in greater detail. Dovetails' overheads have increased over the year from £399,718 to £482,307. Expressed as a percentage of sales, however, these amounts represent a reduction from 20.1 to 19.9 per cent.

To a certain extent, that is to be expected – according to how far the overheads in question are fixed (in the sense that they would not normally be expected to vary with the level of sales or production) or variable (in so far as they would be expected so to vary). Material and direct wage costs will vary directly with the level of production. (Strictly, therefore, these costs should be expressed as percentages of the value of production, not sales. However if it can be assumed that the pattern of sales and production levels are similar – which it often can – sales figures will usually provide an acceptable and more readily available surrogate.) Production and distribution overheads will similarly contain variable cost elements. Some administrative overheads on the other hand – such as office rent – would be expected to remain unchanged regardless of the level of production – at least in the short term and until such time as a threshold is reached at which the increased level of business activity demands, for example, more office space.

An understanding of the nature of overheads – how far they are fixed and how far they are variable – will help in the interpretation of any changes in them which are revealed in the accounts. Frame 35 shows Dovetails' production overheads broken down in more detail. Most of these cost

Frame 35

	19X1 £	19X0 £	Percentage increase	19X1, % of sales	19X0, % of sales
Production overheads					
Consumable tools and stores	49,636	36,697	35.3	2.0	1.9
Hire of plant	16,416	12,210	34.4	0.7	0.6
Depreciation: factory buildings and equipment	41,632	36,092	15.3	1.7	1.8
Repairs and maintenance	25,001	7,464	234.9	1.0	0.4
Supervisory wages	136,021	125,923	8.0	5.6	6.3
Sundry works expenses	22,113	14,257	55.0	0.9	0.7
	290,819	232,643		11.9	11.7

headings will contain both fixed and variable elements and the comparisons are therefore expressed in two ways: first (column 3) as an increase over the same costs for the previous year and second (columns 4 and 5) as percentages of sales for each of the two years.

The two largest increases in Dovetails' production overheads have been in repairs and maintenance (234.9 per cent) and sundry works expenses (55 per cent). While both these costs might to some extent be expected to vary with the level of activity, the increases are wholly disproportionate to the increase in sales (which was 21.6 per cent). As a result, for every £1 generated from sales in 19X1, 1.0p went on repairs and maintenance, whereas only 0.4p was absorbed by these costs in 19X0.

In their attempt to control costs, management should focus not only on percentage increases but also on the size of the overhead in question. Profits are highly sensitive to even a relatively small increase in a large cost: a 1 per cent increase on an overhead of £500,000 will be more damaging to profit than a 20 per cent increase on an overhead of £20,000.

The biggest cost amongst Dovetails' production overheads is supervisory wages. Here management have done well to restrict the increase to 8 per cent. As sales have increased by 26.1 per cent the proportion of the supervisory wage costs to sales has dropped from 6.3 to 5.6 per cent. The figures imply that more or less the same level of supervisory staff have been deployed to oversee an increased level of activity. If Dovetails had allowed their supervisory costs to increase proportionately with sales, the 19X1 operating profit would have been some £17,000, or 13 per cent, less than it was.

By this sort of analysis, management can use their accounts to identify cost changes, assess the causes, evaluate the consequences, and seek to control them in the interests of greater future profitability. For a given level of sales, each £1 of cost saved is £1 extra profit.

Effective cost control needs to be timely. The discussion here is based on Dovetails' annual accounts, but by the time the year-end accounts are ready it may be too late to correct unfavourable cost trends that should beneficially have been recognised much earlier. Astute management will therefore seek to examine their costs regularly and will design their accounting records to provide them with cost information in as much detail as they require. They may arrange that their recording methods provide them with information about the costs and profitability not only of the business as a whole but also of each product or activity that the business is engaged in. Most importantly, management will ask for reports or accounts on a regular – probably monthly – basis. The quicker the information is available, the quicker management can respond.

SALES: CAPITAL EMPLOYED

The attempt to generate more profit from a given volume of sales is one of the two routes to improved profitability. The second route lies in the attempt to generate more sales from a given volume of capital resources.

The discussion here assumes that the *potential* for increasing sales does in fact exist. That potential will depend upon the demand for the product, the company's marketing ability, its sales drive, advertising techniques and all those other aspects of business acumen which would enable Dovetails, for example, to take a greater share of the market for furniture. All of that is outside the province of accounts. What accounts can do is indicate how effectively management are using the resources available to them; they can point to the areas where a more efficient use of capital would lead to greater profitability. In the general attempt to improve the ratio of sales to capital employed, the use of accounts is to focus not so much on increasing the level of sales but on the means of minimising the amount of capital that is tied up in generating those sales.

Dovetails' ratio of sales to capital employed was 2.8 for 19X1 and 2.6 for 19X0 (see Frame 33). Each £1 of capital produced £2.6 of sales in 19X0 and £2.8 of sales in 19X1. Expressed alternatively, Dovetails have had to invest less capital in order to generate the same amount of sales revenue. How has this been achieved, and how can Dovetails encourage the trend? A careful analysis of accounts will help steer management's attention in the right direction. In the same way as sales have been expressed as a ratio of total capital employed, so the various components of that total capital – that is, the various classes of Dovetails' operating assets – can be expressed and compared in the same terms.

Of the total capital employed by Dovetails during 19X0 and 19X1, the bulk of the money was tied up in fixed assets, stocks and debtors. To assess the efficiency with which the company has used its resources we should, therefore, focus on these three major asset categories. The relevant figures from Dovetails' accounts are summarised in Frame 36.

Frame 36

	19X1	19X0
	£000	£000
Fixed assets	488	454
Stocks:		
Raw materials	212	195
Work-in-progress	203	188
Finished goods	20	21
	435	404
Debtors	585	417
Sales	2,425	1,993

FIXED ASSET PRODUCTIVITY

The aim of every business should be to make the fullest use of its fixed assets, and particularly to maximise the proportion of time that plant and machinery is in productive use, rather than lying idle. The ratio of sales to fixed assets provides an indication of how effectively fixed assets have been utilised during the year. Dovetails have achieved an improvement (Frame 37): each £1 invested in fixed assets produced £5.0 of sales revenue in 19X1, compared with £4.4 for the previous year.

Frame 37

	19X1	19X0
	£000	£000
$\dfrac{\text{Sales}}{\text{Fixed assets}}$	$\dfrac{2,425}{488} = 5.0$	$\dfrac{1,993}{454} = 4.4$

The aim should be to push this ratio as high as possible (without of course exceeding the operating capacity of the machinery in question). It should also be remembered that this statistic is based on the historic cost of fixed assets: a ratio based on *current* costs will usually reveal a much less satisfactory return. On the other hand, new machinery would normally be expected to have greater productive capacity, and would therefore generate more output – as long as the demand existed to translate output into sales.

When management make a decision to increase the company's investment in productive fixed assets, they may not expect that investment to show an immediate payoff: the benefits might only be expected to flow after a number of years. In this circumstance the ratio of sales: fixed assets should be assessed over a run of years, rather than merely from one year to the next. More immediately controllable in the short term, and an area which should attract management's continuous attention, is the amount of their investment in working capital.

STOCK TURNOVER

The ratio of sales to stock, sometimes referred to as the rate of stock turnover, is a primary measure of the company's operating efficiency. It also provides a good guide to the liquidity of the company's stock.

The optimum level of stockholding is a matter that requires very careful assessment which can only be decided in the light of the trading circumstances of each individual company. Nevertheless, the *general* aim should be to minimise the amount of money tied up in stocks at any one time, and thereby maximise the rate of stock turnover. A low rate of stock-turn hints at slow-moving stocks, over-buying, or possible obsolesence. On the other hand, an extremely high stock-turn may indicate that the production floor is over stretched, continually flat out, unable to meet demand. The general message bears repetition: ratios or analysis drawn from accounts can indicate changes or trends; it is then up to management to interpret that information, investigate the causes, and evaluate the position in the light of their knowledge of the trading circumstances of the business.

Dovetails' rate of stock turnover has increased from 4.9 to 5.6 (Frame 38): they turned their stock round 4.9 times in 19X0, and 5.6 times in 19X1 – a healthy improvement. This ratio can be adapted to give an indication of the

Frame 38

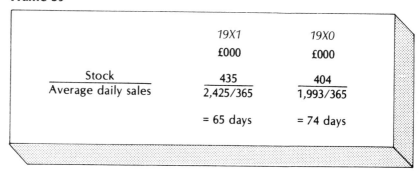

	19X1	19X0
	£000	£000
$\dfrac{\text{Sales}}{\text{Total stocks}}$	$\dfrac{2{,}425}{435} = 5.6$	$\dfrac{1{,}993}{404} = 4.9$

Frame 39

	19X1	19X0
	£000	£000
$\dfrac{\text{Stock}}{\text{Average daily sales}}$	$\dfrac{435}{2{,}425/365}$	$\dfrac{404}{1{,}993/365}$
	$= 65$ days	$= 74$ days

length of time stocks are held on the shelves – see Frame 39. Here it is easier to see that Dovetails are moving their stocks more quickly.

There are two approximations which should be mentioned in this form of stock-turn analysis. First, it is assumed that the level of the stocks held at the year end (and included in the balance sheet) are reasonably reflective of the average value of stock that the company carries day by day during the year. If the level of year-end stock is unrepresentative, management will know the reasons and should take those factors into account in their analysis. The second approximation is that stocks are compared with the revenue from sales: a truer rate of stock-turn will emerge from comparing stocks with the *cost* of sales for the year.

The analysis can be developed – and management can exercise their control with greater precision – by examining the raw material, work-in-progress, and finished goods components of Dovetails' total stock.

RAW MATERIAL STOCKS

Frame 40 compares raw material stocks with the total costs of raw materials consumed in sales during the year (for which see Frame 34).

The result of this comparison shows that Dovetails turned their raw material stock round approximately 5.7 times in 19X0 and 6.3 times in 19X1. Dividing the rate of stock-turn into 365 gives an indication of the number of days' supply of raw material stock that is available on the

Frame 40

	19X1	*19X0*
	£000	£000
$\dfrac{\text{Raw materials consumed in sales}}{\text{Stock of raw materials}} =$	$\dfrac{1,335}{212}$	$\dfrac{1,105}{195}$
Rate of turnover	= 6.3	5.7
Into 365	= 58 days	64 days

shelves. At the end of 19X0 Dovetails had raw material stock sufficient for 64 days' usage. At the end of 19X1, they had the equivalent of 58 days' usage in stock.

It is of course possible to use alternative bases for these calculations. Dovetails could, for example, use the number of working days in the year instead of the full 365 in the calendar. They could compare stocks with the cost of goods produced (rather than sold) during the year. Each basis would produce different statistics. Whatever basis is used, the important point is that it will give a genuine indication of the *trend* of stockholding from year to year (or month to month) and it is the improvement or otherwise in the trend that is of first importance to management.

In general terms, it can be said that the trend of Dovetails' raw material stockholding policy is improving: the rate of stock-turn is increasing. It is less easy to generalise about what is the 'right' amount of raw material for a business to hold. Management will want to hold sufficient at all times to feed an uninterrupted production line. Most importantly, therefore, they will have regard for the expected levels of activity. They will also have regard for the time it takes suppliers to deliver, as well as the possible cash advantages of bulk orders. Good management will usually establish different holding policies for different lines of stock and set minimum reorder levels (and maximum holding levels) for each. Different and sometimes conflicting factors will have to be weighed. The general aim, however, should be quite clear: to minimise the amount of money tied up in raw material stocks at any one time.

WORK-IN-PROGRESS

In Frame 41 the same form of analysis is applied to Dovetails' work-in-progress. Here again the rate of turnover is increasing (from 7.6 times to 8.8 times) and Dovetails are therefore showing an improvement. Under normal conditions (where the pattern of production and sales are consistent over the year) this statistic can give a broad indication of the efficiency of production: the number of days that the average level of work-in-progress takes to pass through the factory. The aim should be to

Frame 41

	19X1	19X0
	£000	£000
Cost of sales	1,786	1,436
Work-in-progress	203	188
Rate of turnover =	8.8	7.6
Into 365 =	41 days	48 days

maximise the efficiency of the production process, to minimise production time and thereby minimise the amount of money tied up at any one time in work-in-progress.

FINISHED GOODS

Frame 42 shows that at the end of 19X1 Dovetails had finished goods in stock which were only sufficient to meet just over four days' sales. Goods are being delivered to customers almost as soon as they come off the production line. Generally, that is an ideal position for a business to be in, although one might harbour some reservations. Dovetails' management

Frame 42

		19X1	19X0
		£000	£000
Cost of sales	=	1,786	1,436
Stock of finished goods		20	21
Rate of turnover	=	89.3	68.4
Into 365	=	4.1 days	5.4 days

will, for example, have presumably assessed the risk of being unable to meet a sudden, unforeseen demand for their furniture. They should also be aware that any future labour or production difficulties – amounting to no more than a few days' lost production – would very quickly put them out of stock, unable to deliver, with the potential loss of customer goodwill.

DEBTORS: SALES

A comparison between sales and stock gives an insight into a company's operating efficiency. The comparison between sales (strictly, credit sales)

Frame 43

		19X1	19X0
		£000	£000
$\dfrac{\text{Debtors}}{\text{Average daily sales}}$	=	$\dfrac{585}{2{,}425/365}$	$\dfrac{417}{1{,}993/365}$
Collection period	=	88 days	76 days

and debtors provides an indication of the efficiency of a company's credit-control procedures.

Frame 43 illustrates how the amount of debtors carried by a company can be expressed as a number of days' sales. The statistic can be interpreted as the average number of days' credit allowed to customers, or the length of time it takes the company to collect its debts. Dovetails' performance in this respect has deteriorated: by the end of 19X1 the company was, on average, taking 12 days longer to collect its money than it was a year earlier.

Taking, £6,643 (£2,425,000/365) as an average day's sales, that is a further £79,700 (£6,643 × 12) of additional and presumably free credit that the company is providing for its customers; and Dovetails are of course having to finance it – by increasing their investment in working capital, for no return.

The company should review its collection procedures, and the terms of credit it presently offers. Management should review the procedures by which debts are reported as soon as they become overdue, so that they can take quick and appropriate action. The aim should be to reverse the recent trend in collection periods, to minimise the average number of days that debts remain outstanding, and thereby minimise the amount of money tied up in debtors.

CONTROL OF WORKING CAPITAL

In analysing Dovetails' profitability, and in using their accounts to pinpoint trends that need to be encouraged or corrected, the emphasis has been on the need to minimise the amount of capital employed, particularly the amount of working capital employed. Control of working capital lies at the heart of profitable performance. It is an area which any businessman ignores at his peril.

In order to illustrate this point, suppose Dovetails have a local competitor, Mortise and Tenon Limited. A year ago, Dovetails looked at the accounts published by M&T and found them to be identical in every respect: the same line of business, the same sales, the same fixed assets, the same amounts of working capital, the same profits and the same profitability.

Frame 44

	Dovetails	Mortise & Tenon
	£000	£000
Sales	2,424	2,424
Cost of sales	1,786	1,786
Cost of raw materials for year	1,335	1,335
Stock, 31 December:		
Raw materials	212	105
Work-in-progress	203	102
Finished goods	20	10
	435	217
Debtors	584	292
Gross working capital	1,019	509
Rate of stock-turn:		
Cost of RM for year: raw materials	6.3 (58 days)	12.7 (29 days)
Cost of sales: work-in-progress	8.8 (41 days)	17.5 (21 days)
Cost of sales: finished goods	89.3 (4 days)	178.6 (2 days)
Collection period:		
Debtors ÷ sales/365	88 days	44 days

A year later Dovetails take a further look at M&T's accounts. They extract information which is summarised in Frame 44 and set against Dovetails' own figures. Once again the two companies are found to be identical in most respects. They have achieved the same level of sales in 19X1 and the same profit margins. The one essential difference is that M&T now have only half the working capital that Dovetails are carrying. Dovetails may think that makes them twice as strong as their competitor. The truth is quite the opposite: they have been only half as efficient.

Dovetails pursue their analysis. They assume the absence of seasonal factors, so that the year end can be taken as being representative of the position at any time during the year. At any one time M&T are carrying half the amount of timber stocks that Dovetails carry. But they are achieving the same level of production and sales, so the timber they do buy they must be using twice as quickly.

Dovetails' calculations support that conclusion: their own timber lies on the shelves, on average, for 58 days before it is used; on the same basis, however, they calculate that M&T's stock waits only 29 days before it is put into production. Similarly with work-in-progress: both companies

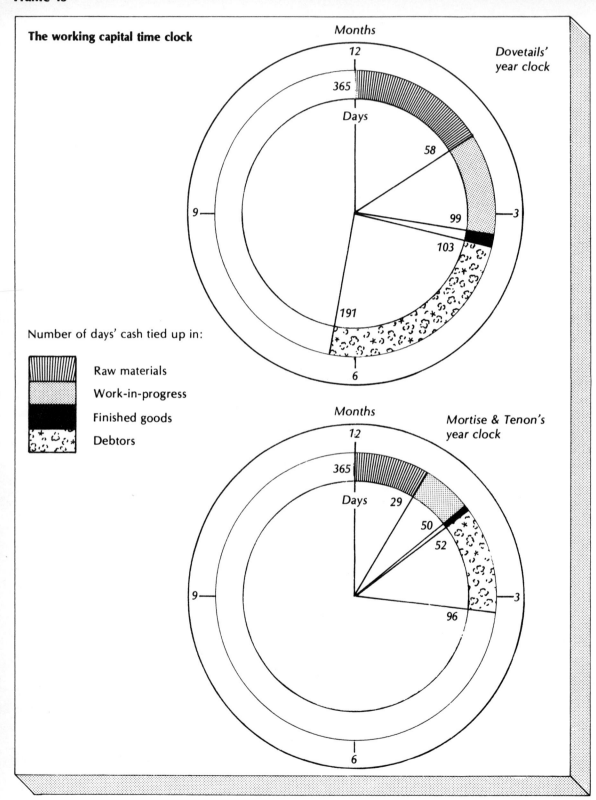

The working capital time clock

Number of days' cash tied up in:

Raw materials

Work-in-progress

Finished goods

Debtors

produce the same amount each year, but at any one time Dovetails have twice as much furniture in the factory awaiting completion; it takes them twice as long to complete the manufacturing process (41 days compared with 21 for M&T). And once it is finished, M&T deliver and sell it twice as quickly – so they only have half the amount tied up in finished goods in the warehouse. M&T also only have half the amount of debtors, because it takes them half the time to collect their money (M&T 44 days; Dovetails 88 days).

To outward appearances the two companies may well look the same. Both will take in the same amount of timber each month and each month both will produce and sell the same amount of furniture. They will have the same level of monthly cash outgoings and both will collect the same amount of money each month from their customers. The difference is simply one of timing.

Frame 45 illustrates the difference diagrammatically. Based on the analysis of their accounts, the money Dovetails pay out for timber remains tied up as raw materials on the shelves for about 58 days. It is then tied up in work-in-progress for the further 41 days it takes to turn it into furniture. It spends four days in the warehouse as finished goods, and a further 88 days locked up in the amounts due from customers. Only then – 191 days later – does it come back to Dovetails in the form of cash.

In contrast, it takes M&T only 96 days to convert cash outflow into cash inflow. M&T can use the cash that flows in on day 96 to buy their next supply of timber; and because it takes them half the time to put the timber into production, and half the time to make the furniture, sell it and collect from their customers, they can go through the whole cycle twice in the time it takes Dovetails to go through it once.

The essence of working capital is that it should be made to work: the harder it is made to work the better for the business. M&T make theirs work twice as hard as Dovetails, and they therefore only need to use half as much of it. There is no better illustration of the saying that time is money.

The extra time they are taking, and their unnecessarily large working capital, is indeed costing Dovetails money – in at least three ways. First, they are having to devote time and resources to the extra paperwork that is needed to control the movements on twice as much stock, and to chase up twice the number of outstanding debtors.

Second, their inefficiency is costing the company money in terms of lost income. Every £1 unlocked from working capital is an extra £1 of cash available for other purposes. Dovetails started the year with a gross working capital base (stock and debtors) of some £800,000. If it had made the same effort as M&T to reduce that by 50 per cent, the benefit would have been reflected in their balance sheet at the end of the year – in the shape of some £400,000 additional cash. With interest rates upwards of 15 per cent, that money in a full year could earn the company £60,000 additional income.

Third, and most important, the cash that is released can alternatively be used to finance expansion. By the same token, as half the amount of working capital might be used to support a given volume of sales, so the same amount of working capital might be used to support double the amount of sales. With tighter control of working capital, and by halving the time they take to convert cash outflow into cash inflow, Dovetails have the potential for doubling their level of business and doubling their level of profits.

As they presently stand, therefore, M&T's efforts to reduce working capital have put them in a much stronger position than Dovetails. If fashions change, M&T can respond much more quickly: they only have half as much work to clear in the production pipeline and they can get their new styles on the market twice as fast as Dovetails. M&T are therefore more adaptable. They are also less vulnerable: if fashions do change, M&T will be carrying only half the amount of old stock and are therefore exposed to only half the amount of stock write-offs and losses that Dovetails could suffer.

If demand increases, M&T can satisfy it more quickly, and with less strain. At present levels, M&T support sales of £2,424 from a working capital base of £509. If a demand goes up by 50 per cent, M&T will need to increase their investment in working capital by some £250 in order to finance their share of the new market. They could probably do that from their own resources.

Dovetails currently need £1,019 working capital to support the same level of sales. They will need to find another £500 – twice as much as M&T – if they are to expand output and take their share of the new business. Because they already have so much money tied up in working capital, they will probably have to borrow the extra they need. That may prove difficult: banks may be reluctant to lend to a business which has already let its working capital run to such high levels. It will certainly be costly in terms of interest, and costs reduce profits.

All that goes to underline one message: tight control of working capital is essential to business profitability. The aim of every business should be to minimise the amount of working capital needed to support a given level of activity. The best way of keeping constant control of working capital is for the businessman to analyse his accounts – and to listen to what they are telling him.

EMPLOYEE RATIOS

One of the most valuable resources available to a business, but one which is given no value at all in the balance sheet, is its employees. Business performance depends very much on staff performance, particularly on the performance of those involved in production on the shop floor and those engaged in selling to the market.

The behavioural aspects of management are, of course, a very significant element in labour relations, and an increasingly large body of theory is now devoted to the effectiveness of different forms of incentive, the motivating influence (or otherwise) of budgeted targets, and the benefits of employee participation. The purpose here is not to discuss the general question of motivation, but to suggest some of the ways in which accounts might be used to assess how effectively management are using the employee resources at their disposal.

The ratio of value of production to direct factory wages, for example, offers a measure of the value produced for each £1 wage cost, and will provide an indicator of whether shop floor productivity is improving or declining. Caution is needed when interpreting the figures. A falling trend does not necessarily imply an inefficient workforce; a decline in productivity might equally result from poor-quality materials, or from machinery break-downs. Nevertheless, with proper evaluation, the productivity ratio is a useful measure, and one which could be of potential interest, for example, to the parties on both sides of a wage negotiation.

Similarly, the ratio of sales to salesmen's wages gives a measure of the amount of sales generated by each £1 spent on the wages of those employed to sell. Here again, the trend in the ratio reflects not only on the efficiency of salesmen but also on the effectiveness of management in motivating salesmen to higher levels of performance, thereby generating higher levels of sales from a given wage bill.

Employee ratios can of course be expressed in terms of numbers of employees rather than wage costs. In either case, comparison of the ratios with those for other businesses should only be made with great care. Productivity ratios will fluctuate significantly according to whether the business is capital- or labour-intensive. For comparable businesses the statistics will be influenced by the conditions in which the workforce are expected to work, and the quality of the plant and machinery they are expected to work with. For businesses in the same trade, the ratio of total payroll to number of employees can, however, provide a useful comparison of average wage levels. Carefully and sensibly used, employee ratios have an important part to play in the control of business performance.

SUMMARY

The profitability of a business depends on both the amount of profit derived from a given volume of sales and the amount of sales generated from a given volume of capital. To improve profitability management's objectives should be to maximise profit (and sales) and to minimise capital employed. Analysis of accounting information provides indicators by which management can assess how far their objectives are being achieved – see Frame 46.

Frame 46

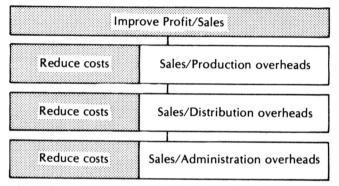

The profit achieved on a given volume of sales can be improved by increasing selling prices (subject to competition and elasticity of demand) or by reducing costs:

Improve Profit/Sales	
Reduce costs	Sales/Production overheads
Reduce costs	Sales/Distribution overheads
Reduce costs	Sales/Administration overheads

The relationship between sales and capital employed can be improved by increasing sales (if demand and productive capacity exists, and profit margins can be maintained) or by reducing capital employed:

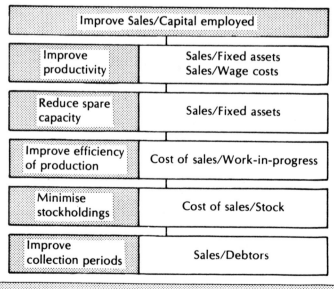

The calculation and interpretation of these and other indicators has been explained in the preceding text. The final two objectives listed – to minimise stockholding levels and to improve collection performance – will also be relevant to an assessment of business liquidity, as described in the following chapters.

10 Analysis for business managers – liquidity

TRADE CREDIT

For most businesses, the amount locked up in working capital can be reduced by taking credit from suppliers. Ideally a business would work off zero working capital – by taking extended credit from suppliers and using the cash collected from customers to pay for the materials.

The investment in working capital can also be reduced by working off a bank overdraft, but whereas credit from a supplier is usually free, money borrowed from a bank is costly in terms of interest.

Once a business starts taking credit, the need to monitor and control working capital becomes even more acute. The use of trade creditors and even bank overdrafts to support working capital may be sound business strategy but it does of course also create liabilities. Liabilities have to be paid, and for the business manager they bring the further task of ensuring at all times that the business has sufficient liquid funds to meet its debts as they fall due.

The potential conflict between minimising working capital and maintaining sufficient liquidity is illustrated in Frame 47.

Assuming an even pattern of buying, throughput and selling, a comparison between trade creditors and average daily raw material usage will give a bearing on the degree to which a business is extending or reducing the period of credit it takes from suppliers. On this basis, Dovetails are now taking some two weeks' additional credit: they presently wait 126 days before making payment, whereas a year ago they were paying within 109 days. That may be good in terms of minimising working capital: as Dovetails take more credit from suppliers, so less of its own money is needed to finance a given level of stock. But with the company now taking upwards of four months to settle its accounts, suppliers themselves will be concerned to assess Dovetails' liquidity position, and management will have to be vigilant in ensuring that there is always sufficient cash to satisfy those creditors who are pressing for payment. The higher the level of creditors, the greater the risk of the company over-extending itself, defaulting on payment, and losing its credit rating. Once suppliers start to lose confidence a business can very quickly find itself in severe difficulties – with creditors all pressing for payment at the same time and not enough money to satisfy them.

It is important to recognise that a profitable business will not necessarily be a liquid one: profits can be represented by, or be invested in, assets other than cash. Profitability is important, but liquidity is critical. In the long

Frame 47

		19X1	19X0
		£000	£000
Trade creditors / Cost of raw materials/365	=	462 / 1,335/365	330 / 1,105/365
Credit taken	=	126 days	109 days

term, a business cannot survive if it is unprofitable; but problems of liquidity do not have a long term – they are usually immediate. A great number of businesses may have the potential for making large profits, but only the liquid ones survive to make them.

A number of the ratios and analyses described in earlier sections have a bearing on liquidity and will help the businessman in his control of it. The average collection period for debtors and the rate of stock turnover tell as much about the relative liquidity of stocks and debts as they do about the efficient use of resources. The emphasis in preceding pages, however, has been on minimising the amount of funds tied up in working capital – converting cash outflow into cash inflow as quickly as possible – and constantly reinvesting it in the working capital cycle. In terms of liquidity, the emphasis is on the sufficiency of liquid funds *at any one point in time*, and for that purpose the main indicators will come from the balance sheet.

CURRENT RATIO

The current ratio results from a simple comparison between current assets and current liabilities. On the basis that the cash to pay current liabilities (by definition payable within one year) will come from the funds generated by current assets (by definition convertible into cash within one year), the ratio provides a broad measure of the ability of a business to meet its short-term obligations.

The ratios for Dovetails are shown in Frame 48. The trend is worsening: at

Frame 48

		End of 19X1	End of 19X0
		£000	£000
Current assets / Current liabilities	=	1,046 / 641	850 / 452
Current ratio	=	1.63	1.88

31 December 19X0, Dovetails had £1.84 of current assets to cover each £1 of current liabilities; at the end of 19X1 they had £1.63 to cover each £1 owed.

The current ratio is, however, only a very arbitrary measure of liquidity. It does not take into account the different degrees of liquidity of the various types of current asset. The cash tied up in Dovetails' raw material stocks, for example, may not be available for another six months, but that may not be soon enough if suppliers are pressing for payment.

Neither is it the case that a high current ratio is necessarily a sign of good business health. A surplus of current assets is a good and necessary thing, but an excessive surplus – particularly if it is represented by old stock and ageing debtors – merely suggests that the control of working capital has been neglected.

QUICK RATIO

A better measure of current liquidity is the quick ratio, which excludes stock from the comparison of current assets and liabilities. By expressing the cover for current liabilities only in terms of cash or near-cash (debtors), the quick ratio provides a more immediate indication of short-term liquidity.

The figures for Dovetails are shown in Frame 49. In these terms the company is almost as liquid as it was a year ago. Traditional benchmarks

Frame 49

		End of 19X1 £000	End of 19X0 £000
Current assets, less stocks / Current liabilities	=	611 / 642	446 / 453
Quick ratio	=	0.95	0.98

were that a company should seek to maintain a current ratio of 2.0 and a quick ratio of 1.0. By that standard, Dovetails' quick ratio of 0.95 compares very reasonably.

Here again, however, the business manager should beware of placing too much reliance on a single statistic. A quick ratio of even 10.0 will give no indication of continuing liquidity if all available cash is needed urgently to replace plant, or if large long-term borrowings are known to fall due for repayment in a year's time. The quick and current ratios calculated from accounts give a first indication of financial health, but good management will assess these statistics in the round of information they can glean from other parts of the balance sheet, in their knowledge of the forthcoming transactions and requirements of the business, and in terms of their ability or otherwise to turn stock and debtors into cash as quickly as possible.

At best, therefore, ratios extracted from annual accounts provide no more than a broad indication of the general trend of liquidity. Unfortunately, the liquidity sickness – when it strikes – strikes very quickly, and the business manager who looks to no more than his year-end accounts will usually find that they tell him too little too late. The cure is to inject more cash, but sufficient cash cannot always be found in time. Even if it can be found, it will usually prove to be very costly medicine. The best form of cure is prevention, and the best way of preventing a liquidity crisis is to prepare cash-flow forecasts.

CASH-FLOW FORECASTS

A cash-flow forecast is the most effective means by which a businessman can plan to ensure that his business will always have sufficient funds to meet its debts. It is a technique which no businessman can ignore. Cash-flow problems are not unique to unprofitable businesses; indeed the very danger of the liquidity crisis is that it can strike at the most successful businesses, particularly those which are expanding.

At their 19X1 levels of operation, Dovetails presently incur the following amounts of monthly cash payments (the figures are based on their 19X1 accounts and are rounded for simplicity): £110,000 to suppliers for materials; £40,000 on direct wages; £42,000 on overheads. Each month they collect approximately £202,000 from customers. The company is generating a healthy cash surplus each month of £10,000.

They have a good order book, so that they plan to operate at the same levels for at least the first six months of 19X2. They start the year with £26,000 in cash and, because they are overdrawn £112,000 against a bank facility of £200,000, further funds of £88,000 are available from the bank should they be needed. The company is profitable and financially sound.

On 1 January 19X2, a new customer makes a large order. The first delivery – for goods worth £60,000 – is for the end of June. The customer will pay cash on delivery, and the price will give a better than average profit margin. It will mean increasing their monthly output by 25 per cent from February onwards, but management assess that they can rearrange the shifts and keep the factory running for 10 hours a day instead of 8. The order is accepted: 25 per cent more business means 25 per cent more profit. The directors are delighted. The truth is that by accepting the order they run a great risk of going out of business before the end of May.

Frame 50 shows the cash-flow forecast that Dovetails should have prepared at the beginning of the year. If they had done so, they would have seen that they would use up their bank overdraft facility in less than five months' time.

Increasing production by 25 per cent will mean spending 25 per cent more

Frame 50

Dovetails' cash-flow forecast 19X1							
£000	Jan	Feb	Mar	Apr	May	Jun	Jul
Opening balance	– 86*	– 76	–110	–144	–178	–212	–186
Cash receipts	+202	+202	+202	+202	+202	+262†	+262
Cash payments	–192	–236	–236	–236	–236	–236	–236
Closing balance	– 76	–110	–144	–178	–212	–186	–160

* Overdraft £112 less cash £26
† Including £60,000 from first delivery of new order

Frame 51

Monthly cash outgoings		
	On existing level of business	On increasing production by 25%
	£	£
Materials	110,000	137,500
Wages	40,000	50,000
Overheads	42,000	48,500
Total	192,000	236,000

on materials each month (suppliers demanded COD for the additional deliveries) and 25 per cent more on wages. Because some overheads are fixed, total overheads should not increase proportionally (the new work is therefore even more profitable). In fact, Dovetails expect overheads to increase by £6,500. In total, accepting the new order will cause the company's monthly cash outgoings from February onwards to increase from £192,000 to £236,000 (Frame 51). However the higher level of receipts will only start to flow in from the end of June. In the meantime, the old level of business is only generating a monthly surplus of £10,000, and existing resources soon expire. The company will exceed its overdraft limit in May. Unless it acts quickly there will be no money to pay creditors, or to pay the wages.

As a result of accepting the new order Dovetails have had to increase their investment in working capital by £176,000 (£44,000 for each of the four months February–May) before any of the extra cash begins to flow back in June. Dovetails then start to reap the benefits, and from then onwards the liquidity position becomes increasingly better. The problem is that the company may not survive until June.

With proper planning, Dovetails would have no difficulty in arranging for a temporary increase in their bank overdraft, or for a payment on account from their new customer. Alternatively, they could seek ways of generating the needed funds internally – by improving their stock turn-round or the collection performance from their debtors – in order to be able to finance the increased level of business from their own resources. With no planning, and no cash forecast, the shortfall in May remains hidden. The irony then is that the company should not take on the new order: they simply cannot afford to be so successful.

SUMMARY

See Frame 52.

Frame 52

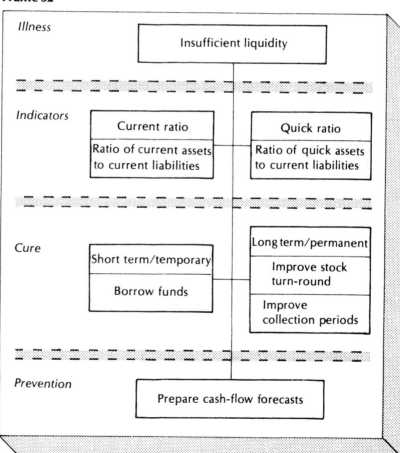

11 Analysis for business proprietors

For the sort of company of which Dovetails is typical, the directors will usually be shareholders in the business as well as managers of it. As well as using accounting information for management purposes, they will also want to use accounts as a basis for examining the worth of their personal investment. The following sections describe methods by which proprietors can analyse their accounts in order to assess the relative profitability of their investment and the degree of risk that attaches to it.

RETURN ON EQUITY

In the same way as the return on capital employed has been used as the primary measure of overall business performance, so the return on their equity provides the first basis from which proprietors can assess the relative profitability of their investment.

When calculating the overall return on capital employed, the comparison was between the full amount of resources available to management (from whatever source they were provided) and the full amount earned from the use of those resources (before accounting for any return on them – whether by way of dividends to shareholders or interest on debt).

For present purposes, however, the definition of capital is limited to the funds provided by Ordinary shareholders and excludes those provided from long-term borrowing. The relevant measure of profit is the amount available for Ordinary shareholders, after interest on borrowings and any other prior claims have been satisfied.

At the beginning of 19X1, the shareholders' funds (share capital plus reserves) included in Dovetails' balance sheet amounted to £639,373. The return earned on those funds during the year – represented by profit after tax and interest, and after extraordinary items – was £61,755. Dovetails return on equity for 19X1 is therefore:

$$(£61,755/£639,373) \times 100 = 9.7\%$$

On every £1 of equity, Dovetails have earned 9.7p. By comparing that return with market interest rates, or with the returns available from other forms of investment, proprietory shareholders can assess how effectively the company has used the equity funds available to it, which itself provides a measure of the relative profitability of their investment.

EARNINGS PER SHARE

A further measure of equity investors' earning potential is provided by the amount of earnings per share. The calculation is based on profit after tax and interest, but before extraordinary items, divided by the number of Ordinary shares in issue. Extraordinary items are excluded because of the distorting effect they have on year-by-year comparisons. The figures for Dovetails are shown in Frame 53. The 19X1 earnings are a considerable improvement on those for 19X0.

Frame 53

		19X1	19X0
		£	£
Profit after tax and interest, and exceptional items	=	61,755	62,810
Number of Ordinary shares in issue		120,000	120,000
Earnings per share	=	51p	52p

For companies listed on the Stock Exchange, earnings per share serve as a major indicator of performance, and have a direct bearing on the market's assessment of those shares. Dividing the earnings per share into the quoted market price provides what is known as the price/earnings or P/E ratio. If Dovetails were listed and their shares were quoted, say, at £5, their 19X1 earnings per share of 67p would indicate a P/E ratio of 7.5 (£5 divided by 67p). If the share price went up to £8 the P/E ratio would be 11.9: the shares would be said to be selling at 11.9 times earnings. Market prices are of course influenced by a great many different factors, some of them totally unrelated to the company's performance. Nevertheless the P/E ratio provides the primary indicator of the level of risk which the market attaches to the investment in question.

DIVIDEND COVER

In many respects, therefore, the trend of a company's earning per share over a number of years – and the estimates which might then be made from that trend as to its likely earning power in the future – act as a major influence on the current price of the shares, and therefore on the value of an investor's shareholding.

A second influence, and one which is regarded by many analysts as being equally important, is the company's dividend record. Regardless of the level of profits that have been generated for equity shareholders, an investor will be concerned also to receive some form of immediate distribution of those earnings as a tangible return on his investment. In particular, he will want to assess the likely level of dividends to come in the future. The relationship between the amount of the company's earnings

Frame 54

		19X1	19X0
		£	£
Earnings available for Ordinary shareholders / Dividend paid	=	61,755 / 21,600	62,810 / 20,400
Dividend cover	=	2.9 times	3.0 times

and the amount distributed is usually expressed as the level of dividend cover.

Frame 54 shows the calculations for Dovetails. The 19X1 dividend is covered almost three times, as was the dividend for 19X0.

The extent of the cover provides an indication to shareholders both of the company's ability to pay out a dividend from current earnings and their willingness to do so. A high level of cover implies that the company can maintain its present dividend with comfort and at the same time provide a supporting cushion from which dividends might be more comfortably maintained in the future. Low cover suggests the company is straining to provide a tangible return to investors and casts greater doubt on the ability to maintain dividend levels in the future. The likely future level of dividends should not, of course, be assessed simply on the basis of one year's payout ratio. Profits accumulated and retained from previous years remain available for subsequent distribution and the amount of reserves shown in the balance sheet will be very relevant to any assessment of future dividend streams. A company's dividend policy will usually be evident from the pattern of dividends over a number of years, and particularly from the relationship between the dividends paid and the earnings available each year. It is notable, for example, that in the last two years Dovetails have paid out only about one-third of their available earnings – implying that they were not concerned to maximise the immediate return to shareholders but preferred to retain a substantial proportion of profits within the business to finance its future expansion. That of course is also to the advantage of shareholders, who may sacrifice income in the present but who then have the prospect of income in the future which is enhanced by the growth of the business.

INTEREST COVER

A matter of major concern to the investor is the degree of risk that attaches to his investment. That risk comes from two main sources: business risk and financial risk. Businesses within the same trade may vary in the general volatility of their profits but that element of risk – the predictability or otherwise of the future flow of profits – will apply to some extent to all businesses which operate in the same sector.

The degree of financial risk, on the other hand, is something which is specific to a particular company. It arises from management's financing policy: the choice between equity and debt as a source of funds.

One measure of the degree of financial risk is given by the calculation of interest cover: a comparison between the interest charges payable on debt and the level of profit from which that interest is funded. In Frame 55, Dovetails' profit before interest and tax is divided by the £12,600 interest paid on long-term borrowings (which is 9 per cent on the unsecured loan stock of £140,000). The interest charge is covered 11.3 times. In 19X0 it was covered 11.7 times. That indicates a very low level of risk to the equity investor: at its present levels of profit, the company is easily able to meet the prior charges on debt and still have a very healthy surplus available for retention or for distribution to shareholders.

Frame 55

		19X1	19X0
		£	£
Profit before interest and tax	=	137,777	157,826
Interest on long-term borrowings		12,600	12,600
Interest cover	=	10.9	12.5

The number of times interest is covered is a statistic which is also very relevant to business managers. As the level of profits becomes low in comparison with fixed interest charges, so proportionately less profits are available from which to provide a return on equity. In the longer run, a low and deteriorating level of interest cover implies that the company is increasingly exposed to the risk of defaulting on interest payment – with the consequent threat of foreclosure.

For these reasons the level of interest cover will also be a matter of first importance to existing lenders – whether they be banks, debenture holders or, as in Dovetails' case, unsecured loan stock holders. Just as importantly, it will be the first point of reference for potential lenders. A company with already low levels of interest cover will find it increasingly difficult to borrow more money; if they do succeed in attracting funds, they will certainly have to pay higher rates of interest on them – in order to compensate lenders for the higher level of risk that attaches to their loan.

GEARING

The comparison between interest costs and the available return on equity is one measure of a company's gearing. Gearing is more usually expressed as the ratio of debt to equity, as measured by the amounts of long-term borrowings and shareholders' funds in the company's balance sheet. It provides an indicator of the company's financing policy: the extent to which management have preferred to finance their long-term requirements from borrowings rather than shareholders' funds.

Dovetails' gearing is calculated in Frame 56. The ratio has fallen from 37 per cent in 19X0 to 35 per cent in 19X1. Note, however, that the figures used for borrowings include amounts representing deferred taxation (£99,107 for 19X1 and £94,900 for 19X0) in addition to the £140,000 unsecured loan stock. Dovetails have not in fact increased their fixed-interest borrowing during the year, and for a profitable company (with growing reserves) that should result in a declining gearing ratio.

Frame 56

		19X1 £	19X0 £
Long-term borrowings / Shareholders' funds	=	239,107 / 679,528	234,900 / 639,373
Gearing	=	35%	37%

The inclusion of deferred tax may not rest easily in this context: there is at least some doubt that it will ever have to be paid, and it is certainly a liability which is very different in nature from loan stock. Nevertheless, it is included in the sense that it represents medium-term borrowing from the Inland Revenue, albeit interest-free.

Other bases, apart from the quirk of deferred tax, are sometimes used to define gearing: for example the ratio can alternatively be expressed as the proportion of borrowings to the total of shareholders' funds *plus* borrowings (which will of course give lower percentages); and overdrafts can, if appropriate, be included in the amount of borrowings (which will increase the percentages). The important point, whatever basis is used, is the trend which emerges from year to year.

Once again the key word is risk. High gearing means high risk – for both lenders and equity investors. Potential lenders will demand a relatively higher rate of interest from a company which is already highly geared. As the gearing and the interest burden increases, so the risk attached to equity earnings also increases: with a higher interest burden, a company will have to make larger profits before any money is available to pay dividends to investors. In return for the higher risk they carry, equity investors will expect a higher than average return when the profits start to flow.

The question of gearing is therefore a matter of the greatest importance to management. Their aim should be to achieve the best mix of capital at the minimum cost. That in turn will require a careful assessment of the expected rates of return on both debt and equity and an awareness of how, for example, an increase in the cost of debt can cause corresponding increases in the expected return on equity.

Nevertheless, any difficulty there might be in establishing the optimum capital mix for a company should not be allowed to blur the basic advantage of gearing. If a business can earn a better return than the rate it has to pay, then every £1 borrowed will increase profitability.

Suppose Dovetails can earn a return of 16 per cent on the capital they employ in the business, and that they presently have equity totalling, say, £5 million, and borrowings of £1 million on which they pay 15 per cent interest. On a total capital employed of £6 million, 16 per cent gives an overall return of £960,000; £150,000 goes on interest, leaving £810,000 for ordinary shareholders – a return on equity of 16.2 per cent. The 1 per cent turn on borrowed money serves to 'gear up' (the North American phrase is 'leverage') the return on equity.

In that example Dovetails have only a modest level of borrowing, and are therefore only moderately geared. Nevertheless a 4 per cent increase in overall return (20 per cent on £6 million = £1,200,000) would result in a 30 per cent increase in earnings for equity (a return of £1,050,000, instead of £810,000, on £5 million). That is the benefit of gearing.

The effect is even more dramatic as the gearing increases. Suppose Dovetails restructure their capital to a gearing ratio of 5:1, £1 million equity and £5 million debt. The overall return of 16 per cent is the same, but a far higher proportion – £750,000 – now goes on interest. That still leaves £210,000 for shareholders on an investment of £1 million – a return of 21 per cent. If overall profitability now goes up by 4 per cent, profits available to shareholders increase to £450,000 – a 115 per cent increase in return on equity! High gearing means high risk, and high risk sometimes brings high reward.

Of course it can also bring disaster. If profits had fallen instead of increasing by as little as 4 per cent (to £720,000), the company would be unable to meet its interest payments out of current earnings. They may be able to draw on reserves for one year, but if the lower rate of profitability continues for any time the company will soon be insolvent. A highly geared company is highly sensitive to even relatively small fluctuations in profit. It is also highly vulnerable to changes in interest rates. A 4 per cent increase in the borrowing rate would wipe out Dovetails' profit.

Gearing is therefore critically important to the businessman – both as a business manager in his search for the most appropriate sources of finance, and as a proprietory shareholder who is concerned with the security of his investment.

VALUE OF A BUSINESS

Gearing also has an immediate and direct bearing on the question of how much a business is worth. An immediate response to that question might be to go to the latest set of accounts. Dovetails' balance sheet at the end of 19X1 shows total assets of £918,635, financed by £679,528 shareholders' funds and £239,107 borrowings.

The first question that arises is therefore whether we are concerned with the total value of the business or only the value of its equity. An assessment of the total worth of the business might start from £918,635 total assets. An assessment of equity value starts from £679,528, i.e. the amount of assets that remain after all borrowings have been repaid. Dividing the amount of shareholders' funds by the number of shares in issue (120,000) gives a figure of £5.65, which could be described as the net asset value per share.

It must be said, however, that for the purposes of valuing a business a set of accounts is not very helpful. Total value or equity value is one question; the next is whether the business is to be valued as a going concern, or whether its worth is to be based on break-up values. The book value of Dovetails' work-in-progress, for example, is based on costs incurred to date. It may well be appropriate to use that figure in a sale as a going concern but, if the business is to be broken up, the half-finished furniture represented by work-in-progress would probably be worthless.

Even in terms of a sale as a going concern, it is very doubtful whether balance sheet values will add up to a reasonable assessment of the worth of the business. The purpose in Part One of this book was to emphasise the fact that although accounting principles provide a useful and valuable framework in which to draw up a set of accounts, they do also act as limiting factors on the type of information that accounts are intended to convey, and they do therefore impose limitations on the alternative uses to which accounts can be put – including the question of the worth of a business. Dovetails' property, for example, is included in the balance sheet at a value of £245,923. That value is based on original cost. The value of the property now could be several times that figure. Similarly with plant, which is included at a residual cost based on an annual depreciation rate of 15 per cent. On the occasion of sale, there may be good cause for reassessing the remaining useful life of plant and machinery, which in turn would lead to revised assessments of their present worth to a potential buyer.

The valuation of a business is therefore fraught with uncertainty. It is even more fraught if we begin to consider the range of intangible factors that can have a bearing on the price at which a buyer and a seller might agree. They include the reputation of the product, the state of the order book and the share of the market the business commands. Those sort of considerations will help build up a picture of the likely future flow of profits – just as much as will the figures reported in any past sets of accounts. And all of that will go to support any figure for goodwill – over and above the values recorded in a balance sheet – which a seller might want to ask and for which a buyer might be willing to pay.

Other influences on the value of a business will include the quality of management, the level of their expertise, the industrial relations record of the business, and the extent to which any development programmes have laid the ground for future commercial growth. And of course there is the question of gearing: a highly geared business is more risky, and will be a less favourable proposition for a potential buyer.

For these sorts of reasons the valuation of the business is one of the more creative financial arts. For companies listed on the Stock Exchange, an alternative method of valuation – but one which is no less influenced by the whole range of imponderables – is through the quoted market price. 200,000 shares in issue, for example, at a current market price of £3 per share gives a market capitalisation for the company of £600,000. But of course this only represents the summation of numerous small holdings: the value of control of the whole business may be worth 50 to 100 per cent more than that figure, as 'takeover' bids have so often demonstrated.

Frame 57

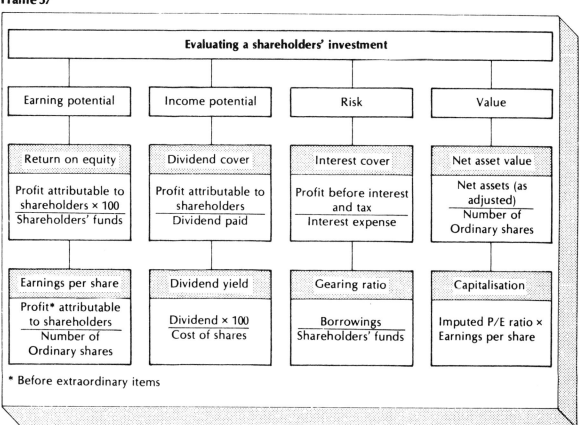

A variation on this method of valuation is frequently used to value the equity in a company like Dovetails. Dovetails' earnings per share in 19X1 were 67p. Reference to the P/E ratios of listed companies in the same business sector might produce an average P/E ratio of say 10. That average would then be (somewhat arbitrarily) adjusted to reflect the lesser marketability of shares in a non-listed company. Further adjustments would be made according to the size of the holding that is being acquired: substantial mark-downs for small, minority holdings; less so as the percentage acquired increases towards a controlling interest, i.e. more than 50 per cent. Whatever the case, applying an adjusted P/E of, say, 7.5 to Dovetails' current earnings per share would give a value for each share of £5.02. That compares with a net asset value per share of £5.65. (In times of high interest rates and yields it is not unusual for a business to sell at less than its so-called 'net asset value'.) The point around those two figures at which a deal might be struck is then a matter for informed guesswork, and clever bargaining.

SUMMARY

See Frame 57 (page 115).

Part Four

POLICIES AND 'PERFORMANCE'

12   Introduction

One of the purposes of this book has been to underline the extent to which the preparation of a set of accounts – and the reading they give of a business's performance – is subject to a considerable degree of estimation and opinion. This chapter reverts to the general question of accounting principles and the alternative methods by which certain of the items appearing in a set of accounts might be arrived at. Its particular relevance will be for those who wish to use accounts in order to assess the strength and profitability of other companies – whether that be small, remote shareholders assessing the company in which they have invested their savings, or a businessman who is looking at another company with a view to acquisition. The fairness of the story told in the accounts will depend very largely on the fairness of the accounting policies which have been adopted in preparing them. The ability to assess the fairness of the adopted policies requires both an awareness of 'standard practice' – in the areas where that has been established – and an awareness of the possible alternatives in those areas for which no one generally accepted method of accounting has yet been developed. This chapter points to some of the items in accounts to which anyone reading them should pay particular attention.

13 Accounting Standards

The number and scope of accounting standards published by the profession in recent years has been substantial. Their purpose has been to narrow the areas of difference between the methods previously adopted by different companies to account for similar items.

There is no doubt that the issue of these statements has enhanced the level of comparability between different companies' accounts: not only are companies now required to disclose the accounting policies that they have adopted, but they are also required to disclose and explain any deviation from standard practice. In addition, the requirement for consistency ensures that the accounts of any one company will be readily comparable – in terms of the bases on which the figures are drawn up – from one year to the next. Nevertheless it would be spurious to suggest that a particular, uniform method of accounting can always be developed to meet the variety of different circumstances in which different types of business operate. The level of uniformity achieved by the issue of accounting standards is constrained by the need to accommodate different business circumstances: for this reason a number of standards have been drafted in order to allow a degree of flexibility and choice.

ASSOCIATED COMPANIES An associated company is one in which the holding is less than 50 per cent (more than which would make it subsidiary), but which is sufficient to give the investing company 'significant influence' over the associate. Significant influence is measured by the extent to which the investing company participates in the policy decisions of the associate. The standard benchmark is that significant influence is presumed to exist where the holding is 20 per cent or more, although the possibility of significant influence arising from holdings of less than 20 per cent is acknowledged.

The assessment of whether or not the company is an associate is therefore a matter of some judgement. The accounting consequences are considerable.

Whereas income from investments would normally be accounted for on the basis of dividends received, the standard treatment for associated companies has been for the investing group to include in its own profit and loss account its full share of the profits of the associate – regardless of whether or not those profits have been distributed. An amount equal to that share of profits is added to the value at which the investment is shown in the balance sheet.

The reader should therefore be aware of the extent to which the company's own performance has been enhanced by its participation in the profits of associated companies. Associated company profits only increase funds available to a company if they are paid up by way of dividend: although the investing company may influence the distribution policy of the associate, it will not be able to control it. Those profits are therefore of a different order to the profits that the company has generated for itself and their degree of significance in the profit and loss account should be read in that context.

EXTRAORDINARY AND EXCEPTIONAL ITEMS

The distinction between extraordinary and exception items – and the impact their alternative treatment can have in the profit and loss account – has been referred to in Part Two. Traditionally, this was a difficult and subjective area. More recently the definition of extraordinary items has been redrawn so tightly as to make them virtually extinct. For the future, therefore, all unusual costs or revenues will be included, as exceptional items, above the line for profit on ordinary activities. Instances of extraordinary items reported below the line in published accounts will be very rare indeed.

LEASING

Largely because of favourable tax treatment, the incidence of leasing amongst companies as a means of financing their operations has grown significantly in recent years. Because the lessee company did not have legal ownership of the assets in question, usual accounting practice had been to omit any mention of the assets in the balance sheet and to account only for the annual rentals in the profit and loss account.

This choice – between leasing and outright purchase – and their alternative accounting treatments led to severe difficulties of comparison between companies. Two identical companies could appear to be quite differently profitable if the capital employed by one included assets that it had purchased while the capital employed by the other excluded any amount for the cost of similar assets which it happened to have leased. Nevertheless the lessee company will by the terms of the lease often have committed itself to leasing commitments of significant amounts for a number of years.

For some years standard accounting practice has required that where the terms of a lease substantially transfers all risks and rewards of ownership of an asset to the lessee, the leased asset should be capitalised in the balance sheet and the corresponding liability included to reflect the future commitments.

PENSION COSTS

The provision of pensions can amount to a significant element of a company's costs, and they are costs the measurement of which involve a very high degree of estimation. The central difficulty is in assessing what level of present costs will be sufficient to fund the benefits due to employees in later years. That assessment involves critical assumptions regarding future levels of inflation, future levels of salary, the expected rate of return on pension fund investments and the life expectancy of employees. Although much of this will be a matter for actuarial assessment, the question of whether a company's present contributions are at a level which is sufficient to meet its future liabilities can have a critical bearing on the profit and loss account. Unfortunately – and perhaps not surprisingly in view of the enormous difficulties of measurement which are involved – the matter of present contributions and future commitments is one to which companies have tended to give little disclosure.

The principle of the relevant accounting standard is that 'the employer should recognise the expected costs of providing pensions on a systematic and rational basis over the period during which he derives benefit from the employees' services'. Several different actuarial methods of valuation are recognised and permitted under the standard. While the standard undoubtedly increases the information disclosed about a company's pensions accounting, it remains to be seen whether it will lead to greater comparability in the accounting treatments adopted.

RESEARCH AND DEVELOPMENT

Until the issue of an accounting standard, the variety of methods by which companies treated their research and development expenditure were numerous. For the most part, R & D costs are intangible and the question as to whether any future benefit will derive from them is particularly intractable. The relevant accounting principle is one of matching: if a cost is not to be written off as an expense to the profit and loss account, then it must be carried forward as an asset in the balance sheet. The consequence for accounts is that any reluctance to write off R & D costs increasingly leads to the accumulation of an asset from which the future benefit to be derived is at best uncertain and at worst spurious.

Standard accounting practice distinguishes between expenditure on pure research (the advance of knowledge), expenditure on applied research (directing pure research towards commercial possibilities) and expenditure on specific development projects (work directed at the introduction or improvement of a specific product or process). No tangible benefit can immediately be related to research costs and therefore they should be written off as incurred. With regard to development costs, however, where there is a clearly defined project and where its ultimate commercial viability can be assessed with reasonable clarity, it is permissable to carry them forward as an asset to be matched against the revenues they will help to generate in the future.

STOCK

The valuation of a company's stock at the balance sheet date is a matter that affords a great deal of room for subjective judgement. Part Two describes how Dovetails' stock was valued by reference to the actual cost of producing it - without reference to its replacement cost or subsequent resale value – and how the choice of 'costs' from the range of different purchase prices during the year significantly affected not only the value of stock but also the calculation of profit. Reference was also made to the level of estimation and opinion involved in those instances where stock is written down to less than its cost, c.g. in order to provide for obsolescence.

Standard accounting practice established some of the ground rules that should be adopted in valuing stock. Nevertheless, it is a good example of the way in which an accounting 'standard' can do no more than establish some basic rules, without attempting to be prescriptive in the more detailed aspects of valuation in order to permit the flexibility which different businesses will need to fairly value totally different types of stock and work-in-progress.

The basic principle is that the costs to be included in stock should be limited to those expenses which have been incurred in bringing the stock to its present condition and location at the balance sheet date, subject only to the general rule that stock should be stated at the lower of cost and net realisable value. The methods that should be adopted in arriving at that cost are not prescribed, other than that they should be those which are most appropriate to the circumstances of the business in order to arrive at an approximation of actual cost. Companies vary greatly in the level of information they disclose and, amongst the difficulties confronting any reader of accounts, two particular problems will be: assessing the method that has been used to arrive at cost; and assessing the extent to which overheads have or have not been included in the valuation.

Alternative methods used to arrive at cost include:

Fifo method

Average cost

Standard or unit cost

Retail prices less average sales margin

Base stock

LIFO method

All of these are methods adopted in order to arrive at an approximation of actual cost. The FIFO method (first in first out) attributes later material costs to stock valuation (and earlier costs to the cost of goods sold). The LIFO method (last in first out) attributes earlier costs to the valuation of stock in hand. The method by which estimated profit margins are deducted from selling prices is one that is used primarily by retail stores.

The following figures summarize the extent to which companies in a recent sample provided more specific information as to their policy for including overheads in stock valuation, and the sort of description which they gave:

Frame 59

	%
Production, works or manufacturing overheads included	49
'Appropriate' overheads included	23
Administrative overheads included in addition to manufacturing overheads	3
All overheads specifically excluded	2
No information given	23
	100

With regard to long-term contracts, standard accounting practice permits work-in-progress to be valued, in given circumstances, at more than cost, i.e. to recognise a proportion of profit before the contract is completed. For companies engaged in this sort of work the estimates of what the eventual profit might be and how much of it can reasonably be recognised in the current year will be subject to a good degree of uncertainty; but those estimates will be critical to the reported results.

DEPRECIATION

The level of judgement inherent in assessing the annual charge for depreciation expense – and its consequence for accounts – has been covered in Part Two. The relevant standard is a further example of an accounting standard which can do no more than establish the basic rule: all assets which have a finite useful life should be depreciated over the accounting periods expected to benefit from their use; the method of calculating depreciation – and in particular the expected life of a particular asset – will be a matter on which different companies will have different views. This again is an area in which the reader – in his attempt to assimilate information from accounts – is largely at the mercy of the willingness or otherwise of the particular company to provide further detail: some companies offer precise and detailed statements of their depreciation policies; others provide information in only the very broadest of terms. In general, the reader should be aware that the older the assets then, in times of inflation, the more understated will be the cost of using them, i.e. the depreciation expense, compared with what those costs would be if the assets needed to be replaced at current prices.

**GROUPS:
CONSOLIDATION**

The Companies Acts include the requirement that, in addition to separate accounts for each individual company, the existence of a group of companies under common control should be recognised by producing consolidated accounts that combine the separate accounts of each member of the group. (A holding company controls another (subsidiary) company if it owns more than 50 per cent of its equity share capital.)

The process of consolidation is one whereby the assets and liabilities of each member of the group, and their profits or losses for the period, are aggregated into one figure in the accounts for the group as a whole. For the most part, the accounts for an individual company, although there are one or two adjustments which are made on consolidation in order that the group accounts portray a fair picture of the financial position and performance of the group *vis-à-vis* the outside world. Thus any amounts due to or from companies within the same group are eliminated on consolidation (because as far as the outside world is concerned no such assets or liabilities exist) and any trading between group companies is excluded from the combined figures for turnover and profit on the basis that a profit only accrues to the group as a whole when a sale is made to external third parties. That apart, there are two further areas of accounting which have particular relevance in the context of groups – goodwill and foreign currencies.

GOODWILL

Goodwill is a term used to describe the amount paid in order to acquire any rights or facilities (such as the right to sell or produce a product, or the acquisition of business connections or 'know-how'), or an amount paid in excess of the value of any tangible assets acquired. In a group context, goodwill will usually arise in the consolidation process in so far as it represents the surplus paid on the acquisition of a subsidiary over and above the value ascribed to the subsidiary's net assets at the time of acquisition.

One point which should be made quite clear is that, where it appears in a balance sheet, the amount shown against goodwill is not an estimate of the total 'goodwill' attaching to the business concerned. A balance sheet is very largely an accumulation of costs incurred by a company: a company may possess a good number of other 'assets' (its workforce, its market reputation, its management skill) which never appear in a balance sheet because accounts do not attempt to put any value on them. It should be underlined, therefore, that the appearance of goodwill does not mean that the balance sheet purports to reflect the value of the business – in the sense of what could be obtained for it if it were sold as a going concern. Goodwill in accounting terms is no more than the amount paid in the past in order to acquire some intangible benefit.

The alternative accounting treatments for goodwill have been various. Some companies have taken the view that, once it has been acquired, goodwill is maintainable and should continue to be shown in the accounts at its original cost, unless there is evidence that its value has been permanently impaired. The alternative view – and one which is supported by prudence – is that balance sheets should not be confused by including assets of dubious or intangible value. The compromise position is that goodwill is an asset which has a finite life, which eventually expires, and which should therefore be written off over a number of years – although that number is something which is totally at the discretion of the company concerned.

Under current legislation and accounting practice only two treatments are permitted: either immediate write-off in the year of acquisition or, if capitalised, systematic write-off over its estimated useful economic life. If goodwill is capitalised, the amount written off each year should be charged to the profit and loss account. Note, however, that where goodwill is eliminated immediately on acquisition, the write-off should be made direct to reserves – thereby avoiding the profit and loss account altogether.

FOREIGN CURRENCY TRANSLATION

Where a group has overseas subsidiaries, the problem arises as to how the operations of the foreign company are to be translated from the local currency into sterling for inclusion in the UK consolidated accounts.

Different methods of translation are possible, and it is an area of accounting for which it has proved difficult to establish any one generally accepted treatment. Accounting standards have established it as standard practice in most circumstances to translate overseas profit and loss accounts at the average rate of exchange ruling during the year and to translate overseas balances at the closing rate of exchange ruling on the balance sheet date. (An alternative treatment would be to translate foreign currency assets and liabilities at the rates ruling at the time each transaction was entered into.) Because of wide fluctuations in foreign currency exchange rates, the differing methods of translation can have a marked impact on the results disclosed by a group with significant overseas operations.

More importantly, there have been alternative views as to how any differences that arise from the translation process should be treated in the accounts – in particular, whether they should be included in the profit and loss account or accounted for direct to reserves. Current practice is that exchange rate differences that have no cash flow implications for the company concerned should not be allowed to distort its reported results for the year. Thus the 'differences' that arise merely from the accounting process of expressing figures recorded in one currency into the domestic currency have nothing to do with the operating performance of the group (unless and until overseas profits are repatriated, i.e. funds are transferred from one currency to another) and should not therefore be reflected in the profit and loss account but taken direct to reserves.

Whether the process of translation will result in a 'profit' or 'loss' in any one year will depend on how sterling has moved against the particular foreign currency during the year in question. The reader should therefore scrutinise the method by which the company has dealt with these differences: it has not been unknown in recent years for companies to switch their accounting policy in this respect according to whether or not the movement in sterling has given rise to a 'profit' on translation (in which case it becomes attractive to account for that profit in the profit and loss account) or a 'loss' (in which case the reasons for accounting direct to reserves becomes more persuasive).

Appendix 1 Glossary of terms

Accounting bases
The (sometimes alternative) methods that have been developed for applying basic accounting concepts to business transactions and for measuring certain items in the accounts, e.g. various methods for depreciation of fixed assets.

Accounting concepts
The basic assumptions underlying the preparation of accounts, including 'going concern', 'accruals', 'consistency' and 'prudence'.

Accounting policies
The specific accounting bases judged by the business to be most appropriate to its circumstances and therefore adopted in the preparation of its accounts, e.g. of the various methods of accounting for depreciation, the policy adopted may be to depreciate plant plant over a five-year period.

Accounting records
The 'books' in which a business records the transactions it has entered into. For companies, minimum standards of accounting records are required by law.

Accrual
An expense or a proportion thereof not invoiced prior to the balance sheet date but included in the accounts – sometimes on an estimated basis.

Accruals concept
Income and expenses are recognised in the period in which they are earned or incurred, rather than the period in which they happen to be received or paid.

Advance corporation tax
The tax a company is required to pay (at the basic income tax rate) when it makes a distribution. The amount paid can be subsequently set off against the company's corporation tax liability for that year.

Asset
Any property or rights owned by the company that have a monetary value.

Balance sheet
A statement describing the financial position of a business at a particular date.

Capital allowance
An allowance against profits given for tax purposes in respect of expenditure on fixed assets.

Capital employed
The aggregate amount of long-term funds invested in or lent to the business and used by it in carrying out its operations.

Capitalisation	The treatment of costs as assets to be included in the balance sheet rather than as expenses to be written off in the profit and loss account.
Cash flow	A statement – often a projection – of future, anticipated cash balances based on estimated cash inflows and outflows over a given period.
Consistency concept	The requirement that once an accounting policy for a particular item in the accounts has been adopted the same policy should be used from one period to the next. Any change in policy must be fully disclosed.
Contingent liability	A liability dependent upon the outcome of a future event.
Costs of goods sold	Those costs (usually raw materials, labour and production overheads) directly attributable to goods that have been sold. The difference between sales and cost of goods sold gives a measure of gross profit.
Creditors	Amounts due to those who have supplied goods or services to the business.
Current asset	An asset which, if not already in cash form, is expected to be converted into cash within twelve months of the balance sheet date.
Current liability	An amount owed which will have to be paid within twelve months of the balance sheet date.
Current ratio	The comparison between current assets and current liabilities in a balance sheet, providing a measure of business liquidity.
Debentures	Long-term loans, usually secured on the company's assets.
Debtors	Amounts due from customers to whom goods or services have been sold but for which they have not yet paid.
Deferred asset/liability	An amount receivable or payable more than twelve months after the balance sheet date.
Deferred taxation	An estimate of a tax liability payable at some estimated future date, resulting from timing differences in the taxation and accounting treatment of certain items of income and expenditure.
Depreciation	An estimate of the proportion of the cost of a fixed asset which has been consumed (whether through use, obsolesence or the passage of time) during the accounting period.
Distribution	The amount distributed to shareholders out of the profits of the company, usually in the form of a cash dividend.
Dividend cover	The relationship between the amount of profit reported for the year and the amount distributed.

Dividend yield The relationship between the amount of dividend per share and the market share price of listed companies.

Double entry A system of bookkeeping whereby the amount of each transaction the business enters into is recorded in two places – according to the manner in which the transaction increases or decreases any one or more of the business's assets, liabilities, capital, revenue, or expenses.

Earnings per share The amount of profit (after tax, but before any extraordinary items) attributable to shareholders divided by the number of Ordinary shares in issue.

Exceptional item Income or expenditure that, although arising from the ordinary course of business, is of such unusual size or incidence that it needs to be disclosed separately.

Expense A cost incurred, or a proportion of a cost, the benefit of which is wholly used up in the earning of the revenue for a particular accounting period.

Extraordinary item Any significant amount of income or expenditure arising from events outside the ordinary activities of the business and which, because of its unusual nature, needs to be separately disclosed.

Fixed asset Assets held for use by the business rather than for sale.

Fixed cost A cost that does not necessarily vary with changes in the scale of operations, e.g. rent.

Gearing The ratio of debt to equity, usually expressed as the proportion which long-term borrowings bear to shareholders' funds.

Going concern concept The assumption that the business will continue in operation for the foreseeable future, i.e. that there is no intention to curtail or significantly reduce the scale of operations.

Gross profit The difference between sales and the cost of goods sold.

Historic cost convention The convention by which assets are valued on the basis of the original cost of acquiring or producing them.

Interest cover The relationship between the amount of interest payable during a period and the amount of profit (before interest and before tax).

Liability An amount owed.

Liquidity A term used to describe the cash resources of a business and its ability to meet its short-term obligations.

Listed investments   Investments the market price for which is quoted on a recognised Stock Exchange.

Long lease   A lease with an unexpired term in excess of 50 years.

Long-term liability   An amount payable more than twelve months after the balance sheet date.

Materiality   A subjective judgement of the extent to which any amount is significant in the context of the financial position of a business as described in the balance sheet or its reported profit or loss.

Net assets   The net amount of total assets less total liabilities.

Net book value   The cost (or valuation) of fixed assets less accumulated depreciation to date.

Net realisable value   Amount at which an asset could be sold in its existing condition at the balance sheet date, after deducting any costs to be incurred in disposing of it.

Nominal value   The face value of a share or other security.

Overhead   An expense that cannot be attributed to any specific part of the company's operations.

Post balance sheet event   Any event occurring after the balance sheet date, but before the accounts are issued, which is sufficiently significant to be either reflected or noted in the accounts.

Prepayment   The part of a cost which is carried forward as an asset in the balance sheet to be recognised as an expense in the ensuing period(s) in which the benefit will be derived from it.

Price/earnings ratio   The relationship between the latest reported earnings per share and the market price per share.

Prior year adjustment   A retrospective adjustment to the previous years' accounts which is reflected by revising comparative figures in the current year's accounts.

Profit   The difference between the revenues earned in the period and the costs incurred in earning them. A number of alternative definitions are possible according to whether the figure is struck before or after tax, extraordinary items, distributions, etc.

Profit and loss account   A statement summarising the revenues earned and the costs incurred in earning them during an accounting period.

Provision   The amount written off in the current year's profit and loss account in respect of any known or estimated loss or liability.

Prudence concept

The philosophy which says that when measuring profit provision should be made for all known or expected losses and liabilities, but that revenue should only be recognised if it is realised in the form of cash or near-cash.

Quick ratio

The relationship between those current assets readily convertible into cash (usually current assets less stock) and current liabilities.

Reserves

The accumulated amount of profit less losses, and any other surpluses, generated by the company since its incorporation and retained in it.

Revenue

Money received from selling the product of the business.

Share capital

Stated in the balance sheet at its nominal value and (if fully paid, and subject to any share premium) representing the amount of money introduced into the company by its shareholders at the time the shares were issued.

Shareholders' funds

A measure of the shareholders' total interest in the company, represented by the total of share capital plus reserves.

Share premium

The surplus over and above nominal value received in consideration for the issue of shares.

Statement of Standard Accounting Practice

Statements issued by the accountancy bodies which describe approved methods of accounting. (*Abbrev.* SSAP.)

Tax credit

The amount of tax deducted at source (at the basic rate of income tax) by a company from any dividend payment.

Timing difference

An adjustment to accounting profit in order to arrive at taxable profit which arises from the difference between the accounting and taxation treatment of certain items of income and expenditure.

Turnover

Revenue from sales.

Variable cost

A cost that increases or decreases in line with changes in the level of activity.

Working capital

Current assets less current liabilities, representing the amount a business needs to invest – and which is continually circulating – in order to finance its stock, debtors and work-in-progress.

Work-in-progress

Goods (or services) in the course of production (or provision) at the balance sheet date.

Index

capital allowances on, 54–5
depreciation of, 36, 37–40
productivity of, 89–90
replacement of, 39–40
tangible, 36–7
valuation of, 40
freehold property, 39, 59

gearing, 53, 112–14
'going concern', idea of, 27–8
gross margin, 62–3, 84–6
gross profit, 62–3

'historic cost' principle, 25–6, 40, 82

information, useable, 76
interest cover, 110–11
investments, 40–42

liabilities, 18–20, 21; *see also* current liabilities
liquid funds, net, 70
liquidity, 102–7
  cash-flow forecasts, 105–7
  current ratio, 103–4
  quick ratio, 104–5
  trade credit, 102–3
long-term loans, 52–3

'matching' principle, 26–7, 43

objectives of management, 99–101
operating profit, 63, 82
ordinary shares, 53, 57, 108–9
overheads, 46, 86–8
  production, 87–8

performance, measuring, 24–5
plant/machinery, 27, 39–40
preference shares, 53
prepayments, 47–8
price/earnings (P/E) ratio, 109, 116
profit, 20, 23, 26–7, 80
  gross, 62–3
  operating, 63, 82
  ratio to sales, 84
  retained, 59, 110
profit and loss account, 20–3, 29, 61–6, 80, 85
  dividends, 65–6

'extraordinary' items, 64–5
gross profit, 62–3
operating profit, 63
taxation, 63–4
turnover, 62
profitability, 80–101
  elements of, 83–4
proprietors, analysis for, 108–16
'prudence' principle, 28–9

quick ratio, 104–5

ratios, 76
  current, 103–4
  debt: equity, 112–14
  debtors: sales, 93–4
  employee, 98–9
  price/earnings of shares, 109, 116
  profit: sales, 84
  quick, 104–5
  sales: capital employed, 88–9
  sales: fixed assets, 89–90
  sales: stock, 90–91
raw materials
  costs of, 43–5
  stocks of, 91–2
'realisation' principle, 25, 26, 28
Registrar of Companies, 57
reserves, 58–9
return
  on capital employed, 82–3
  on equity capital, 108
revenue, 20–23, 25
  reserves, 59
risk, business/financial, 110–13

sales
  ratio to capital employed, 88–9
  ratio to debtors, 93–4
  ratio to fixed assets, 89–90
  ratio to profit, 84
  ratio to stock, 90–91
share capital, 56–8
share premium account, 58
shareholders, 50–51, 56–8, 66, 108, 110
  evaluating investment of, 115
shares
  earnings per share, 109